The Sales Manager's Success Manual

WAYNE M. THOMAS

American Management Association

New York • Atlanta • Brussels • Chicago • Mexico City • San Francisco
Shanghai • Tokyo • Toronto • Washington, D.C.

Special discounts on bulk quantities of AMACOM books are available to corporations, professional associations, and other organizations. For details, contact Special Sales Department, AMACOM, a division of American Management Association, 1601 Broadway, New York, NY 10019.
Tel.: 212-903-8316. Fax: 212-903-8083.
E-mail: specialsls@amanet.org
Website: www.amacombooks.org/go/specialsales
To view all AMACOM titles go to: www.amacombooks.org

This publication is designed to provide accurate and authoritative information in regard to the subject matter covered. It is sold with the understanding that the publisher is not engaged in rendering legal, accounting, or other professional service. If legal advice or other expert assistance is required, the services of a competent professional person should be sought.

Library of Congress Cataloging-in-Publication Data

Thomas, Wayne M.
  The sales manager's success manual / Wayne M. Thomas.
       p. cm.
  Includes bibliographical references and index.
  ISBN-13: 978-0-8144-8050-2
  ISBN-10: 0-8144-8050-0
 1. Sales management.   2. Selling.   I. Title.

  HF5438.4.T46 2008
  658.8'1--dc22

                                          2007021977

Printing number

10 9 8 7 6 5 4 3 2 1

With love to my wonderful wife Susan for her encouragement, insights, assistance, and perseverance. God has given me a great partner and mother for our children, Kathryn and Emily.

Contents

Preface

He who is not prepared today will be less so tomorrow.

OVID

Ralph Waldo Emerson observed, "a person is what he thinks about all day long." Our business associates see us clearly and react to us accordingly.

I worked at IBM with a short, fat, bald man with a round face and glasses. He wore a perpetual grin atop his perpetually rumpled suit. Bill was not the person you would pick out of a lineup as the top salesperson in the branch. However, he was.

I also worked with John at IBM. He worked like a dog, attentive to every wish of his customers. His suit was pressed. He had a ready "hello" and willingly lent an ear to anyone who needed one. Yet, he was our branch Willy Loman, habitually near the bottom in sales.

What was the difference between Bill and John? John worked under rain clouds. You could read him as a victim all the way across the office. He was late (or lost the deal, or came in second, or had insufficient support) because of heavy traffic (or a sick child, or an overzealous competitor, or requirement to help his wife). The ever-present strain on his face showed him in a constant combat with all of life's exigencies, large or small.

In contrast, Bill refused to allow circumstances to rub that wide grin off his face. He just never gave up. You could see it in that smile—even when he was in big trouble. I would kid him that he could be in a room with water rising up to his nose, and would keep grinning because he knew without doubt that he would somehow prevail because he knew if he persevered somehow the plug would get pulled.

Bill saw himself as a winner; John as a victim. It was obvious to all of us. Is the lesson here that the difference between winning and losing is this simple? Do you succeed because you act, as Emerson implied, from positive beliefs all day long?

Bill and John worked for the same company under the same compensation plan, had the same training, worked for the same manager, and began their careers with equal opportunities. They also faced situations typical for anyone in sales: aggressive competitors, economic ups and downs, and products that were sometimes a less than an ideal match for their customers' needs.

Bill and John are not unusual. In your own experience as a sales manager or Chief Sales Officer (CSO), you have seen Bill and John many times with different names. Their difference is in their attitude. John sees himself as a victim of circumstances. Bill comes through despite circumstances by flowing with them, surmounting them, going around them, ignoring them. He works with the reality that things are what they are.

This book is about succeeding in the face of challenging circumstances commonly encountered in sales management. *The Sales Manager's Success Manual* is a sales manager's coach, providing you tools and strategies to work with what you find. What you add is your own mindset.

Part I is about taking your team to market. These chapters (1 through 9) focus on the important elements of that process. The aim is to help you identify potential problems that can derail you and to provide tools and ideas to address them.

Part II is personal coaching for you. In these chapters (10 through 21) we provide methods and tools to help you make better decisions, understand the drivers inside your sales reps' heads, and share practical application of important research to your success as a sales manager.

Sales management is a challenging career, and more so today than ever. Everyone in the job faces complexity, globalization, bigger challenges, and more unforgiving metrics. The most successful sales managers will synergize all the ideas that follow with an outlook of confidence that communicates to others that you are a winner. I encourage you to write me with your results at Wayne@ThomasAndCompany.com. I will respond to your email personally. Thank you for this opportunity to be part of your career plan.

Acknowledgments

I am grateful to the many salespeople, managers, and executives who have influenced my thinking on *The Sales Manager's Success Manual*. My thanks go out especially to Thomas Aebischer, Ray Allieri, William Beaumont, Pasquale Bibbo, John Bleuer, Brian Casto, Steve Clairmont, George DeSola, Sue Heintz, Fred Jorgenson, Richard Lippmann, PhD., William McCormick, Mark McKersie, David McNeff, Daniel Moros, MD, Eric Pettersen, Bob Puissant, Gary Sarmento, Douglas Schongalla, Mark Simon, Matt Stocking, Gary Thomas, Susan Thomas, Alex Walker, Mark Welsh, Deborah Wills, Walter Wilowaty, and Robert Wilson. Of course, no one should suppose that all these people agree with everything I've written.

Wayne M. Thomas

PART 1

Taking Your Team to Market

CHAPTER 1

Going to Market
Leadership and Responsibility

In the last business downturn, to cut costs, companies focused on doing more with less. This challenged sales managers to reduce personnel and increase the productivity of those who remained.

In the latest business upturn, many businesses refocused from cost cutting to growth. This challenged sales managers to increase headcount and goose everyone's productivity to pay for growth.

In the next business downturn . . . well, you can spot the pattern here. Business cycles do repeat, and each time they do, sales managers are challenged to adapt their organizations without delay. It is a critical point often missed, however, that while the major ups and downs may look similar, the required sales management skills are in constant evolution.

In *Death of a Salesman,*[1] Willy Loman laments the good old days of dull competition, account control, and customer loyalty. He tells his sales manager about his idol, who could blow into towns in thirty-one states, check into a nice hotel, put on green velvet slippers, and take orders over the phone. Willy believes selling is now dead. "In those days . . . Howard . . . there was respect, and comradeship, and gratitude in it. Today it's all cut and dried, and there's no chance for bringing friendship to bear—or personality."

The Internet and information-age technology add their own flavors to the constantly changing environmental mix in which companies operate. Companies can wither or shine under the 24/7 spotlights of the information age; the lights shine as brightly on the losers as on the winners. The pressure to win is relentless, and so is the demand for growth. Last month's financial darling may be this month's goat. CEOs and boards who cannot achieve their results honestly take ethical shortcuts and even risk prison to sustain the appearance that they are winners. Behind the real winners, it is the 363,000 men and women in professional sales management, often unsung heroes, who deliver the all-important results that make the boss look good.

"The Ultimately Accountable Job . . ."

In a September 2006 *Harvard Business Review* special sales double issue, sales guru Jerry Colletti described sales leadership as "The Ultimately Accountable Job. . . ."[2] Schering-Plough CEO Fred Hassan observed what sales managers have always known—namely that no company's strategy can succeed without control of its top line.[3] In corporate America, it seems as if sales is taking over the playing field as engineering recedes. Hence, sales is where the big money is today with more than half of sales managers earning six-figure incomes. Sales managers are the top earners of all corporate managers below CEO.

And why not? Sales managers routinely have responsibility for teams producing tens of millions of dollars from single accounts. Today's stakes are higher and the challenges more sophisticated than ever. In all of this, the most successful sales managers will see ripe opportunities for personal, career, and earnings growth.

It Takes a Leader—and Sometimes a Lucky Break

Despite all their emergent visibility and responsibility, CSOs do not have the direct power or resources to assure the results demanded of them. To succeed in a world defined by the decisions of others, they must be masterful leaders, influencers, marketers, financiers, salesmen, and recipients of a few lucky breaks!

Sometimes they look for their breaks outside the rules. The Gallup organization found that more than a third of sales managers knew that their reps lied to make a sale. These managers contributed to consumers' perceptions of sales as at the bottom of consumer honesty and ethical standards.

Realities

CSOs must produce their results within the macro economic, political, technological, regulatory, and competitive environment set by others—nationally and globally.

At the company level, CSOs operate under conditions set by their superiors and peers—who often make decisions with barely a glance at their effect on sales. Take a well-meaning CFO who argues for a cap on individual sales earnings so that finance can budget sales commissions more predictably. He may not understand that he is also killing sales incentive. In another example, Verizon's sales agency program had an unusual feature for more than a decade: When agent companies exceeded compensation budgets, Verizon told its agents they would not be paid and advised them to stop selling!

Often, the CSO has no say in sales decisions. After all, sales neither chooses the products it sells, nor funds its compensation plan, nor controls competition. It does not schedule manufacturing, manage operations, or dispatch service personnel. Sales neither quality checks production nor designs the capacity of plants. It neither determines the company's financial structure nor establishes its purchasing efficiency.

At lower levels within the organization, sales personnel are often in political conflict with others outside of sales. Motives are second-guessed, and envy is common due to the apparent freedom sales people enjoy—let alone their nice sales trips. All this has the effect of diluting a company's integration behind the sales program.

And then, there are the customers. It is not easy to attend their mercurial demands and maintain their (supposed) loyalty while also selling them products and services at a good profit. Even in this age of expensive CRM systems, just 20% of customers are happy with the sales coverage assigned to their accounts.

All of these constraints occur in every sales environment, and they are not necessarily problems. They come with the job—and they are surely surmountable.

Going to Market

The chief sales executive takes the company to market. Eight primary go-to-market elements influence the CSO's world and the world of his or her people. Internal decisions determine four elements. These decisions are changeable, sometimes relatively quickly:

- The sales force
- The sales environment
- Sales controls and policies
- Sales alliances

The other four elements are external decisions driven by

- The product/market match
- Competition
- Customers
- The market

Understanding the Terrain

Success in going to market results from the sales manager's ability to understand the interplay of these eight elements and to maintain a harmony within them adequate to achieve assigned objectives. With misalignment of even one element, a sales program can fail. To emphasize this, I call these potentially catastrophic yet avoidable problems Hindenburg Omens. Finding and defusing them is your first order of business when you take command.

Hence, each of the next eight chapters examines a single go-to-market element so that you can evaluate its adequacy or inadequacy (a Hindenburg Omen) for the success of your program. This is particularly important at the beginning of a new job or promotion into sales management. This follows advice of the famous military strategist Sun Tzu, who wrote in *The Art of War* 2,400 years ago, "As a leader there are few things more important than understanding your terrain." A commander "ignorant of the conditions of mountains, forests, dangerous defiles, swamps and marshes . . . cannot conduct the march of an army."[4]

To help evaluate factors of your terrain, you will find insights from experienced managers, interesting examples to illustrate key points, and fascinating research you can apply practically. You will learn to spot problems quickly, and if you find an Omen, there are solutions and ideas to help you prioritize and manage it.

The Hindenburg

Longer than three Boeing 747s, the 804-foot Hindenburg Zeppelin was the largest manmade airship ever to fly. It was the Titanic of the sky, designed and built with confidence that it was an engineering pinnacle. It was, however, like the Titanic of the sea, spectacularly ill fated.

The Hindenburg was a luxury, hydrogen-filled airship that crossed the Atlantic seventeen times, logging 190,000 miles carrying thousands of passengers in luxury. The airship's designers were so confident in their craft that they positioned a smoking room aboard just below 7 million cubic feet of highly flammable hydrogen.

On May 6, 1937, at 9:15 PM, the Hindenburg began mooring at New Jersey's Lakehurst Naval Air Station. Suddenly, hundreds of people on the ground saw a flash near the airship's tail. In less than one minute, the Hindenburg fell to the ground destroyed by fire.

Sales Omens

The Hindenburg saga has parallels and lessons for sales leaders. For example, past success is no guarantee of the future. Even after seventeen smooth flights across the Atlantic, calamities can occur. To those who examine with the benefit of hindsight, the tragedy will always seem to have been predictable. There may have been a trip-wire awaiting some unfortunate person or event to trigger it. Perhaps the problem was in plain sight and deemed trivial, but grew imperceptibly until, like an avalanche, it crashed down. Whatever the cause, there is always a requirement to fix the blame on those whom it is claimed ought to have foreseen the tragedy.

In sales, you are the one who ought to have foreseen unpleasant surprises. This is why you must flag Hindenburg Omens before they trigger and derail your program. For instance, a high attrition rate of good performers eventually leads to failure over time. In hindsight, this is obvious. However, because the trend occurs over time, it may go unrecognized until it is well established.

Constant Vigilance

Past success may cause managers to become overconfident and dull their awareness of environmental shifts. Becoming less aware of change, they develop blind spots and assure themselves that the good, old ways still hold. For them, this is the beginning of the end. With change itself occurring at an exponential rate, nothing remains static very long. Former Intel Chairman Andy Grove recognized how this tendency grows from success. To guard against it, Dr. Grove put it succinctly, "only the paranoid survive."

Professor Mad Eye Moody in the *Harry Potter* series adds a corollary that survival is the result of "constant vigilance"! These admonitions are good advice for everyone's sake particularly when taking command as a company's new CSO. One of your critical responsibilities is vigilance to find and fix Hindenburg Omens.

Do It Now

Finally, there is a lesson to apply from watching high-profile CEOs take command of troubled companies. The most astute CEOs do all they can to open a clean page in the corporate history book when they first take command. They announce downsizing decisions; sell underperforming assets; make personnel changes; make financial write offs, and even restate prior years' results. They deliver the bad news early and as a package. Savvy new CEOs use their honeymoon period to get all they can behind them, knowing there will never be a more opportune time.

The first Ford Motor CEO from outside the family, Alan Mulally, is a textbook example. Mulally joined Ford in September 2006. The following month he announced a quarterly loss of $5.8 billion, and he said the loss for the fourth quarter would be even larger. He reserved $9.5 to $10.5 billion for restructuring costs, warned of negative cash flow for the next several years, and suggested the sale of Aston Martin, Jaguar, and Land Rover. He said in an early interview, "I came in with my eyes wide open. What's good is we are dealing with the reality now."

Likewise, the lesson for new sales managers is to draw a firm line separating themselves from the misadventures of their predecessors. As Mulally did, build in reality rather than overcommit. The tool shown in Table 1.1 is a handy way to begin.

As you examine each of these major components of the go-to-market process, determine if you find yourself with an element of your program that is "adequate" or "inadequate" to attain your objectives.

This is a simple way to prioritize your work. Since any "inadequate" rating stands in the path of reaching your objectives, these are your priorities. "Adequate" means that the element is OK for now. Explore each area and all its related processes and procedures carefully, so you can thoroughly understand what is required to correct or work around it. To do this, you will find helpful ideas in each chapter.

The table is a triage tool. Its purpose is to quickly sort critical items and identify potential points of failure. When you spot an

TABLE 1.1 Triage Table: Rating Eight Go-to-Market Elements

Element	Adequate	Inadequate/Hindenburg Omen
1. Sales Force		
2. Sales Environment		
3. Sales Policies		
4. Channels		
5. Product/Market Match		
6. Competition		
7. Customers		
8. Market		

inadequate element, you must drill down to all of its component parts. This requires thorough preparation, digging through details, and understanding the situation so well that you become an expert on the issue. Your next step is to educate the CEO about the strengths and weaknesses of the company's go-to-market plan. You are going on record to gain consensus and help, if you need it.

Prepare Thoroughly for CEO Presentation

Sales executives are not famous for mastering the kind of detail that their colleagues in marketing use to nail their points, according to several CEOs we interviewed. Rather, CEOs know sales managers as likely to present anecdotal evidence supported by relatively little research. This puts them in the position of having their case easily challenged. By thorough preparation that anticipates questions and challenges, you will make your point and demonstrate that you are no average sales executive.

There are two main objectives in this preparation. The first is to verify that a problem actually exists and affects your ability to achieve the company's sales objectives. It puts you on record early and provides the greatest possible time to address the inadequate element and turn the sales plan around. Your second objective is to rally commitment and support to align others in the company behind the essential changes required.

Your Leadership in Action

I believe the best way to present your assessment of the company's go-to-market strategy is to use a few simple visuals and tell a story around them. For example, Figure 1.1 shows the key elements of going to market. It visually depicts the key chapters of your story. Use it to show how parts interact to achieve or hinder sales results. It allows you to walk a CEO, board, or your peers through the go-to-market terrain describing what you found. As you move from element to element discussing how everything interacts to create a positive or negative influence, take the opportunity to explain what you have already done or plan to do to make changes or build on the strong capabilities that are already in place.

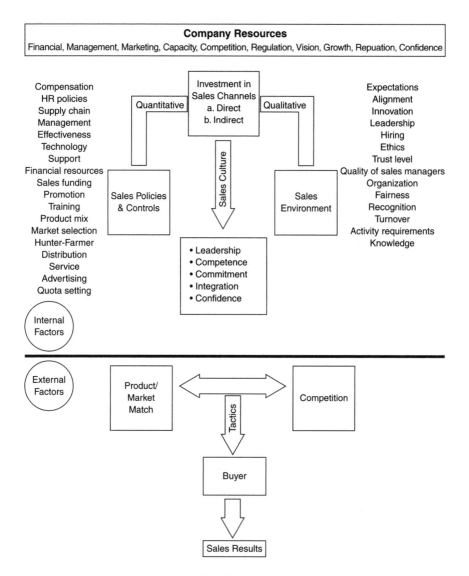

FIGURE 1.1 Forces responsible for sales results.

Upon completion of your session, you have developed a common awareness of the challenges and opportunities you see, described the changes you think are essential, heard suggestions from others, put yourself on record for requesting help where needed, and acquainted everyone with a comprehensive program that won't leave them guessing what sales is doing to achieve its objectives.

Keep your presentation handy for review and update. Let it serve as a reminder of (1) what you found, (2) what you have accomplished, and (3) what others acknowledged, promised, and delivered. Increase the power and interest of your story by using the imagery of the following section: The Path of Least Resistance.

The Path of Least Resistance[5]

"All truths are easy to understand once they are discovered; the point is to discover them."

GALILEO GALILEI

In nature, energy finds and flows along the path of least resistance (POLR) in any structure. A structure acts like a riverbed channeling the water flowing through it. Before Hurricane Katrina in New Orleans, water flowed predictably into the Gulf along its POLR. As a levee gave way, there was a change in the underlying structure. The water always takes its POLR and now will flow over the levee. The new POLR is just as predictable as the old one.

You Can Predict Success or Failure

Likewise, the eight elements of your go-to-market strategy interact to form your unique structure with its own path of least resistance. When you understand this structure, you can determine how it will affect the behavior of your salespeople and your strategy. If the elements of your plan interact to create your desired structure, your go-to-market program will follow the POLR as planned. You can study your structure to predict how changes might affect the POLR.

Remember that the energy of your program is not aware that the underlying structure is good or bad. It simply takes its POLR, as in the following example. As you will see, once you understand the structure, you can predict the behavior (POLR) it will cause.

The CEO pays the head of operations strictly on results of operational objectives. That is, her performance objectives are unaligned with your sales objectives. It is easy to see how this simple structural misalignment may affect your effort to integrate the department's attention with the company's sales strategy.

For instance, you see opportunity for a high-end sale in Atlanta. The CEO tells you to make the sale even though there are no techs there to support it. "Don't worry about it. We'll work it out." How will the operations manager feel about hiring an Atlanta tech that could cost her a quarterly bonus? Will she hire a tech after just one sale? If you were managing operations, when would you hire a tech?

People take their path of least resistance. In this actual case, operations decided to fly in a tech until business built enough to hire one locally. Unfortunately, that was not good enough for the customer, who travels his own path of least resistance, fearing that the proposed arrangement would be inadequate for his company.

Successful sales managers understand conflicts such as this. They understand how an underlying structure channels the behavior of anyone within it. In fact, they can predict it. When they need to change behavior, they do not tell people to buck up and try harder. They know they must change the underlying structure. Only that will change the POLR.

To do this they look for the best leverage points. In this case, if operations had a compensation plan supportive of an expansion strategy to achieve sales growth, we would have seen better alignment of objectives (change in the underlying structure) and thus different behavior (a new path of least resistance).

With all this background information in mind, let us move through the eight elements of going to market, beginning with the sales force.

CHAPTER 2

The Sales Force

*When you get right down to it, one of the most important tasks
of a manager is to eliminate his people's excuse for failure.*

ROBERT TOWNSEND

Most companies find the cost of going to market is their second-largest expense—just behind COGS, the cost of goods sold. Depending on the mix of goods and services, companies may spend up to 40% of revenue marketing their products. As CSO, you are a steward of this investment. In your role, just a few strategic decisions will add to or subtract from the company's return on its investment.

One of your first decisions is whether the current sales force is adequate or inadequate for its mission. Do you or don't you have the right people?

According to Caliper, an organization specializing in recruitment and selection, 80% of salespeople are in the wrong jobs. After a study of 78,000 sales representatives, Caliper concluded that 55% should not be in sales at all, and that 25% were in the wrong kind of sales.

If Caliper's findings describe your salespeople, you have a Hindenburg Omen on your hands. You have also discovered an area where your leadership as an agent of change will make you a valuable corporate asset.

How to Assess Your New Team

How do you determine if your reps and staff are a match for the mission you are leading? You need clarity on two things. The first is your company's objectives, which flow from its mission. The company's mission might be: "To make money for the Hunter family and to cure cancer." More specific objectives flow from that: "Achieve $5 billion in sales this year." Second, you must create a sales strategy to achieve the objective(s). You can only begin your sales force assessment with these ends in mind.

For example, to achieve $5 billion in sales, you decide upon a fundamental change in field tactics. Your new strategy requires a solution selling approach to corporate-level (C-level) executives. In the past, the sales force called primarily at the department level using product-oriented tactics. It was effective, but meeting your new assigned objectives requires high growth in existing accounts. The sales force must expand its skills to include effectiveness at the corporate level. Now, assessing your sales force becomes more straightforward. Do they have the polish and technical expertise to be credible at the C-level? Have they demonstrated it before?

Collecting Data

- Examine the results of existing sales teams and individuals sales reps.
- Socialize your sales vision with colleagues in other departments, and gather their feedback.
- Talk to some of your customers.
- Review team performance with your sales managers, meet one-on-one with top-performing sales reps.
- Review performance reports on sales and team activity.

At the earliest possible time, begin making field calls with your salespeople. There is no better way to make a confident assessment of your terrain than by experiencing it yourself. Do not accept someone else's assessment, because his or her evaluation criteria may be different from yours.

Riding in a car with sales reps always provides deep insights available no other way. After a few days in the field, you will appreciate the sales culture, marketplace, customers, and competition more insightfully than any other way. Then, with the confidence of your own observations, you can make faster, more sound decisions.

Remember that you are taking a small sample of the whole organization as you make your calls. Do not take everything you hear or see as a universal truth. Be aware of what I call "the rep who" influence. Psychologists tell us that we have easy recall of, say, "the rep who" you rode with last week who claimed that the company's tech support was lousy. You must keep an open mind later when the issue of tech support arises, remembering that each of us has a different perspective on the truth. We see through the eyes of one in our personal context. Try to simply flag issues for further investigation rather than assuming you have special insight from that single exposure.

Your early need is to see the big context and make decisions about how the structure you inherit facilitates or inhibits the behavior it does. That said, making sales calls can unearth solutions to great mysteries and provide valuable insights.

I debriefed a new CEO who had returned from a week's worth of sales calls. Primarily, he had called on large accounts and top executives within those accounts. He learned that while the company believed it had a major account program, all it really had was a product sales program. Most of the executives he called upon had no idea of the diversity of his company's products and the potential benefits available by more integrated partnering. This insight led him to develop, despite protests from his VP of sales, a separate major account group under different management.

Do It Now

Many months will pass before the benefits materialize from major sales organization changes. Because of this ramp-up time, a new CSO must determine early if she will make major changes in her channels. This is essential because she also must set expectations early.

In clear terms and wary of overconfidence, the CSO must inform her CEO how much time will be required to ramp to achieve expected results from the change. She must also warn the CEO of estimated productivity declines in the interim. Then she must get a firm commitment of support.

If you don't get buy-in, at least you have put yourself on record assessing the inadequacy of the current sales team to achieve objectives. In denying your request, the CEO also goes on record with you.

What happens next? You begin to limp along with a sales force that you have identified as inadequate to do the job. A smart CEO will be open to reconsider your earlier assessment as it now comes to pass. Inaction will not solve the problem.

Loyalty to one's staff is important; however, loyalty can hurt people who are asked to perform tasks incompatible with their attitudes and skills. You cannot send ducks to eagle school.

A former VP for an international communications firm shared her experience: "The market need these days is for consultative selling. We could have great product-oriented salespeople, but they just wouldn't have the horsepower to do the job required today." Her experience was that 80% of the existing sales force failed to adapt to consultative selling. "There is no time to waste these days. My advice is to make cuts and changes all at once. Loyalty to you isn't worth much if you don't make your numbers." If you don't, it will be your neck on the block.

"You Got to Know the Territory!"

Another sales VP advises new CSOs not to stop with changes to the sales channels. "Also assess political alliances of your staff and field managers." In addition to fourteen years as a sales leader, he has a black belt in karate and is a student of Sun Tzu's *The Art of War.* "I wish I had taken Sun Tzu's advice myself when I became a sales VP—'know your terrain.'" Sun Tzu says that any commander "ignorant of the conditions of mountains, forests, dangerous defiles, swamps and marshes . . . cannot conduct the march of an army."[1] "Only after you understand your terrain can you develop an effective strategy." In other words, you must adapt your tactics to the reality of the environment as you find it. To illustrate, he discussed several managers in technical and administrative positions whom he inherited and knew to have political loyalty to others.

Spies

"They were essentially spies." By the time he learned that several of these holdovers were actively undermining him, it was too late to move them out of his organization. To his chagrin, he discovered that his boss clandestinely maintained an open door to them.

"I should have gotten rid of them immediately and put in people loyal to me. I was reluctant to do that because of their political connections. Now I realize there would have been some of initial discomfort, but it would have been well worth it. In the end, they killed me."

With your own loyalists, you can move earlier and more decisively. Most sales executives believe the optimum strategy is to make your personnel changes quickly. Stringing them out will kill morale and cause your best people to look for companies where shoes are not always dropping.

I know this from personal experience. I was a sales executive brought in to AT&T to help its sales force succeed in a deregulated environment. In this environment, AT&T announced that 40,000 employees would be separated from the company. You can well imagine the internal environment after this announcement.

The downsizing occurred over several years. During that time, morale was low and stayed there. Instead of a focus on market success, the employee focus turned to and remained on personal survival. I observed a sales organization with a short-term, personally pragmatic outlook. Because the downsizing occurred in stops and starts, predictability vanished. Throughout its 100-year history, perhaps more than anything else, predictability of the company's systems, markets, and policies drove the loyalty and commitment of its employees. Thereafter, virtually nothing became predictable, and the culture collapsed. Who could have predicted that the most recognized company in all the world be sucked into decades of decline, finally culminating in the sale of the company?

Assessing the Future

No one would have predicted the demise of AT&T. Because of the market's unflinching confidence in AT&T, it was able to borrow more money than any corporation in the United States and at favorable rates. Did all of its brilliant employees suddenly become inept? No, they simply became victims of a market environment, which changed because of technology, regulation, and competition.

Just because prediction is so difficult does not mean that we should not try. By careful observation, many things are highly predictable. Again, the best time to make your prediction is before accepting the job. There are some good ways to do this:

- Through your networking contacts.
- By interviewing customers.
- Through your interviews with the CEO, peers, and if possible, sales managers.
- By reviewing results.
- By assessing the level of supervision and control in place in the sales organization.

Some CEOs have little feel for the sales department. It is best to know this now to understand whether you will be a good match for each other. With good information and good questions, you should be able to assess your CEO's sales temperature. What is the CEO's policy about compensation? Is he willing to let salespeople and sales managers make big incomes?

Where you identify a highly cost-conscious CEO, you can bet that the sales organization will tend to be undersized. If you determine the need for additional salespeople, would you have his support? As a sales professional, you know that more salespeople make more sales than fewer salespeople. Experience also says that in growing a sales force, it may be better to bring on new reps all at once rather than over time. Most CEOs are unfamiliar with the concept of carryover.

Depending on the sales cycle and nature of the business, up to 40% of next year's business can be directly attributed to selling that began this year. This is the concept of carryover. There is a reason that many CEOs and CFOs do not understand this principle: It is due to the optical illusion that whenever there is a major sales organization downsizing or management change, sales results may appear unaffected—in the short term. Those who do not understand sales do not understand that the continuing sales are the result of work begun months in the past. Fewer reps do not produce as much as more reps. Unfortunately, this myth becomes the problem of the new CSO who inherits a pipeline with insufficient carryover to buoy future results.

Contracting the Selling Activities

One major decision awaiting CSOs is a review of existing partner relationships, or whether some (additional) segment of the sales program ought to be effectively outsourced to indirect channels. These independent companies perform the selling function primarily by extending your company's reach into segments familiar to them and not you. This subject is a book in itself and beyond the scope of this book, which focuses on the direct sales force. Many management parallels do apply, however.

Additionally, there are decisions to be made about the wisdom of deploying other selling technologies such as inside sales and the Internet, to reach additional markets cost effectively.

In the next section you'll find a powerful tool to weigh the question of whether to add more personnel to your sales force.

Sales Channel Sizing and Company Profitability

Make every decision as if you owned the company.

ROBERT TOWNSEND

Cost Containment

Companies are always at work on lowering their cost of goods sold to gain competitive advantage through price reductions or to fatten margins. As you read earlier, sales-related expenses are usually the second largest cost item. In a downturn, some companies also focus on reducing sales expenses and/or improving sales productivity. There is a variety of ways they do this.

Some companies reduce direct and channel costs by a percentage ("15% across the board cut"); some reduce costs through straight funding cuts ("take $2.5 million from the budget"); still others contain costs through controls such as mandating a target ratio of revenue to sales expense ("sales will be 15% of revenue").

However, the three approaches above are financial strategies, not necessarily good sales strategies. Even in difficult times, if the company is in a growth market, none of these strategies may recognize the opportunity to maximize profits.

The analysis in Table 2.1 illustrates—counterintuitively—that sales cost containment limits a company's profitability in a growth market.

Productivity Improvements

Productivity improvement is always in season. Some firms channel expense by purchasing automation software to improve sales productivity. If CRM (customer relationship management) delivers a 10% improvement in sales productivity, there are second-level choices. Is this an opportunity to grow sales without adding headcount? Or is this an opportunity to reduce sales headcount by 10%? In a growth market, the appropriate choice may be to reinvest into sales force growth in order to grow revenue and profits.

Invest in Sales or Reduce Costs?

The analysis in Table 2.1 makes the case to add sales headcount. It also demonstrates for the factors given that containing sales costs in

TABLE 2.1   Current Situation

Results	Rationale
$100,000,000 total sales for last year	77 reps = $1,300,000 average sales per rep
Revenue = 3.7 times the breakeven sales cost per rep	$245,000 loaded cost per rep at 70% GM (gross margin) = $350,000 sales required to breakeven
The ratio of the cost of the sales force to sales is 19%	$18,865,000 sales force cost/ $100,000,000 sales = 18.9%

a growth market will not maximize profits. Sales investment helps maximize profits.

Status Quo.   In Table 2.1, the company makes no changes: The directive to sales is: Maintain 19% sales expense to revenue with no additional sales hires.

Investment for Profit Improvement   In this next example, the directive to sales is: Increase the sales force by eight reps for greater reach and coverage (see Table 2.2).

Observations   The decision to add eight reps increases the sales expense to revenue ratio by 1%, but adds $1,950,000 to the bottom line. This occurs despite sales performance at only 50% productivity (ramp up) their first year at full loaded cost. There is still a safety margin to cover the breakeven cost of the new reps even if sales fell to 30% of the established reps' production.

TABLE 2.2   Improving Profits

Results	Rationale
$5,200,000 in incremental sales	$650,000 sales per rep times 8 new reps. (50% of annual quota due to ramp up, etc.).
1.86 times the breakeven sales cost per person	$350,000 breakeven sales per rep with $650,000 average sales
$1,690,000 incremental sales cost	8 reps at $245,000 loaded cost each
$3,640,000 incremental gross margin	70% of total incremental sales of $5,200,000
$1,950,000 added to company bottom line **profit**	Incremental profit from subtracting total loaded cost from total gross margin
Revenue to sales cost ratio is 20%	$20,825,000 sales force cost / 105,200,000 total revenue = 19.8 %

Consider Carryover

A CFO or CEO could argue that many companies appear to have cut their direct and indirect channel costs with relatively little effect on the current year's production. This can sound like a compelling argument. It is a good argument only in the short term. In the longer term, the company handicaps itself by ignoring sales carryover and market growth.

Recall that sales carryover recognizes that sales made today are the culmination of sales groundwork done in the past, months or even years earlier. It follows that a drop in sales effort today will not show up until months later, perhaps even the next year. Depending on the industry and length of a sales cycle, up to 40% of next year's sales result from the previous year's activity.[2] This phenomenon makes carryover an important planning consideration.

Furthermore, if you are blessed with a growth market, the company loses the advantage it may have gained by securing a larger share. The foregone growth and profits cannot contribute to the company's financial health and competitive position.

Now, you must take all the information you have gathered and weigh it against the task ahead of you. The sales force is either adequate or inadequate to meet the assigned objectives. If the sales force is adequate, it passes the minimum threshold required. Therefore, it will not be an initial priority for you. Of course, everything can be improved, but that is not your task right now. You are looking for Hindenburg Omens. A rating of inadequate signifies a Hindenburg Omen.

In Pursuit of Rewards: Chocolate, Sex, and Money

When I am getting ready to reason with a man I spend one-third of my time thinking about myself and what I am going to say, and two-thirds thinking about him and what he is going to say.

ABRAHAM LINCOLN

Freud saw our minds in constant battle between the forces of rationality (superego) and the forces of "I want it now" (id). When rationality prevails, we are said to display emotional intelligence. We are able to delay gratification. Of course, this is an important power to have, or at the least, to have others perceive that you have it.

We are all familiar with those animal experiments where the lab animals drop from exhaustion after nonstop pushing of control bars to release pleasurable substances. Today an MRI enables us to watch ourselves manage our temptations in living color. Researchers observe that we are often on the edge of performing in irrational ways as the power of our own id skirmishes with rationality.

When emotional intelligence loses, according to Freud, pursuit of rewards can inspire our own worst behavior. Like it or not, we are still evolution in process with many of our animal-brain proclivities in good working order. Freud's observation, confirmed in color by MRI, explains some of the unusual things we see in sales management. Now we know why people act the way they do. Here is a simple example.

Chocolate and Sex

What do attractive people, sex, and chocolate have in common with money? They all activate the same region of our brain that lights up an MRI when a person ingests morphine or cocaine. Just as they react to sex and drugs, your sales reps can become chemically buzzed up pursuing money or receiving it.

"Whether it's reacting to a sexual conquest, a risky business deal, or an addictive drug, the brain often distinguishes clearly between the thrill of the hunt and the pleasure of the feast."[3] For many sales people the chase is reward enough. Sometimes pursuit pushes the rep into risky, unethical, or uncollegial behavior.

Non-Money Rewards

Sales reps do not do what they are not paid to do. Fortunately, researchers Hans Breiter and Daniel Kahneman have demonstrated the power of psychic rewards are a currency, too.[4] Their experiments demonstrated that even salespeople derive pleasure from the hunt whether the payoff is self-esteem, money, or both.

A sales success provides a major high from victory, recognition, and being on top. I saw this principle in action the time my top sales rep won our biggest order ever. In a spectacle right out of *The Music Man,* he marched into our building escorted by a high school marching band. He was smiling and nodding to onlookers like Professor Harold Hill leading 76 trombones!

After the Thrill of the Chase

Of course, the commotion flags when the chase ends. Sometimes, too little interest remains in implementation. This behavior is reminiscent of a classic sales bait and switch joke: During the sales process, the salesperson lavishes golf, exquisite dining, and the promise of perpetual sunshine under blue skies upon the prospect. The rep creates an indelible image of the pleasures and benefits that lie ahead, if only the prospect will sign the contract. He signs and soon discovers that all of this was an illusion. When the customer asks what happened to all the ruffles and flourishes before the sale, the sales rep responds, "yesterday you were a prospect, but today you're just a customer."

Astute Observation

One sales team used this proverbial insight to turn several apparent losses into victories. They encountered a talented competitor named Mike who beat them regularly. They studied him and looked for a weakness, which they found. Mike did not require a signed contract to experience the thrill of victory. All he required was to be told that he was the winning vendor. After that, he appeared to down-shift his activity, even to take a vacation. The result: Weeks passed before Mike negotiated a signed contract.

We realized that this lag time made him vulnerable to stealing his deal. There is always some degree of buyer's remorse with a major decision. Add to this a time lag and the potential for unpleasant surprises lurking in an unsigned contract, and you can see the reason for our hope of turning around an occasional loss.

Perhaps this example is so unusual that you may never apply it. Perhaps the better lesson is this: We need to take every advantage, even small ones, to win. In baseball, the batting champion ekes out every hit he can, because winning the title or a deal may depend upon it.

Viewed in a different context, if you were Mike's manager, you would provide him a valuable coaching service by studying why it takes him so long to reel in his dinner. In the next chapter we will see more ways successful sales managers create a positive sales culture for their teams.

Ethics in Question

In our research interviews with their non-sales colleagues, we heard allegations that "sales will do anything to get the sale." This is another of those "your greatest strength can be your greatest weakness" paradoxes. Sales should do (almost) anything to get a sale that is moral, legal, and ethical. Losing a sale by doing anything less is apostasy!

Not just corporate colleagues question sales' ethics. A Gallup poll of consumers found that of all the business occupations, selling and advertising were ranked at the bottom in terms of honesty and ethical standards.[5]

Sales ethics are not a black-and-white thing. Salespeople are expected to be enthusiastic about their products. However, when does enthusiasm spill over into puffery, white lies, or untruths? Sales management must communicate answers, lest they risk their company's future.

For Met Life and Putnam, questions about sales ethics have prompted internal reorganizations. For Prudential, an ethical charge cost it over $425 million because its sales force oversold clients. Ethical problems at Arthur Anderson, WorldCom, and Enron caused prosecution and bankruptcy. Obviously, ethical problems are not limited to unreliable firms.

The issue is not going away. I say this because ethics have a large situational component. What is unspeakable in one situation can be excusable in another. Is it ever moral to murder your own baby? *U.S. News & World Report* raised this question in an article on moral issues.

Many psychologists believe we have several powerful moral precepts that are hard-wired within us through evolution. It is an emotionally settled issue at first pass that we would never murder our own child. Not so fast, claim a team of Princeton researchers who underscore the role situational elements play in accepting or over-riding our initial gut reaction. Princeton's Joshua Greene proposes that "a moral judgment is ultimately a balance of several different considerations—the initial, primal reaction; empathy; cultural or religious norms; and individual reasoning. Sometimes these will all be in line and make the decision an easy one, but often they will conflict."[6]

The team ran a study posing the following situation: "Enemy soldiers have taken over your village and will kill any civilians they find. You are hiding in the cellar of a house with a group of townspeople, and you hear the soldiers enter the house. Your baby starts to cry, and the only way to quiet him is to hold your hand over his mouth and, eventually, smother him. But if the baby keeps crying, the soldiers will discover your group and kill everyone, the baby included. What should you do?"

In this situation about half the subjects said they would murder their own child. Researchers observed the decision process via MRI and saw the collision of emotion with cognition and conflict control.

Situational pressures will increase on our sales forces as they face more capable global competition and smarter, more demanding prospects. The future of the direct sales job is more uncertain than ever. Reps worry about outsourcing, downsizing, sharing territory with indirect channels, mergers, acquisitions, reduced budgets, and higher quotas.

The most successful sales managers will anticipate these ethical challenges and address them with their teams. They will make their standards clear and define the penalty for unethical behavior. Careers, reputations, and the viability of our companies are at stake.

Keep in mind that personal standards of conduct are usually higher than business standards. Employees often perceive that business behavior at lower standards levels is acceptable. *USA Today,* referencing an article by Susan Powell Mantel,[7] found this perception goes across department lines. They reported that nearly half of all workers admitted in a survey that they had committed "unethical or illegal acts."

It is not just the brains of salespeople that slosh around with potent doses of reward-seeking chemicals. Money and other situational variables seduce corporate workers and create skullduggery in every department.

CHAPTER 3

Sales Environment

One machine can do the work of fifty ordinary men.
No machine can do the work of one extraordinary man.

ELBERT HUBBARD

Of all these go-to-market elements, the one over which the CSO has most influence is the field sales environment. The culture of a field sales office is the living laboratory demonstrating the level of confidence the sales team has in itself and its company. Sales leadership plays the key role in establishing the department's competence, commitment, and credibility with other functional areas.

If the sales team maintains a winning trajectory through its results, the CSO is halfway home. The balance of his effort and that of his managers will be built upon foundational practices that support winning in the long run. Leadership must demonstrate competent decisions in the areas of training, coaching, hiring skill, representing the department's interests to other departments and to senior management, assuring adequate compensation, field support, and ability to maintain a confident sales culture.

Type 1 or Type 2 Situations

A new CSO seeking to turn the tide on an unsatisfactory sales performance should answer two questions about the sales culture before setting her strategy. Is the negative sales spiral because of:

1. Incompetent leadership within the sales department (internal); or

2. Perception of incompetent sales leadership, often the result of poor companywide integration of the sales effort stemming from a company's poor self-confidence, senior management ignorance, or CEO incompetence (external)?

Ostensibly, the company hires a new CSO because the last one didn't work out. This is an incomplete answer, however. The full answer completes the sentence ". . . didn't work out because . . . (usually reasons 1 or 2)." It is important to determine which so that you can address the actual underlying problem.

The perception of sales by others is a good clue about the extent of sales integration into the actions of other departments. When interviewing for a new position, if you hear someone say: "This is an operations-driven company," you can hypothesize a great deal more. "Operations-driven" is a common code phrase for an organization with silos, local power bases, and a CEO who has not well integrated his resources behind the marketing effort. The implication is that you will be at a disadvantage to a competitor whose organization believes that everyone's role is to win customers and keep them close.

In one company, I heard the pricing executive describe the sales managers this way: "They all lie." His boss, the CFO, told me, "I asked them what price he (sic) needed, gave it to them, and then he lost the deal. These guys are incompetent." In a company with such commonplace disregard for sales, you can bet that the CEO is part of the problem, too.

At this company, the CEO had not aligned the objectives and compensation of operations, finance, and sales. Managers were paid for accomplishing their parochial tasks without a single objective—

even total revenue—in common with sales. Further, at the CEO's staff meetings the group sport was pummeling the Sales VP for his missed forecasts. That the CEO allowed this to occur sent a clear signal to everyone reflecting his confidence in the sales executive.

Monkey-in-the-Middle

This senior team sport reminded me of a game my children play called Monkey-in-the-Middle. There are few rules because the game is obvious to everyone. "It" is the Monkey in the Middle and play is easy. Players circle around the monkey and toss a ball back and forth keeping it away from the Monkey-in-the-Middle.

In the business world, sales is often the Monkey-in-the-Middle. Like the kids' game, this monkey-in-the-middle is isolated while all the others circle around in the camaraderie of a management team consisting of everyone but sales. The game is an apt analogy, particularly in seeking the answers above. In fact, as this book demonstrates, when sales revenue is down, sales is often not the cause. Nevertheless, sales is always the easy target to be perceived as the monkey-in-the-middle. The successful CSO finds the truth and collaborates with other senior executives to solve the company's problems. In short, he must know the truth and tell the truth.

Ineffective Outside Intervention

I coached a CSO who was behind in his numbers, but whose biggest job was managing his CEO. His CEO spent more time looking over his shoulder managing sales than in focusing on the survival strategy of the firm. That made it clear to the sales force who really ran the sales force. It also demoralized them. Salespeople are very observant and understand quickly what's going on. They intensely dislike interference from anyone outside of sales.

So, they were not at all happy when the CEO devised a new contest and had it delivered through their VP. This CEO observed that if the sales force closed just 15% more proposals, sales would meets its numbers. Therefore, ask the sales force to raise its proposal win rate to 30%. That may have been a simple observation for the corner office to make, but achieving the result was a different story.

As if by magic, proposal win rates grew to the magic number. Unfortunately, the company did not get a step closer to its targets. How can this be? Salespeople simply delayed reporting losses while continuing to report wins. The term *malicious compliance* was created for the situation like this. The implication is you do precisely what you have been asked to do but absolutely nothing more. To justify a slowdown in loss reporting, sales decided that loss decisions ought not to be made hastily. After all, who knows when a situation could change and provide the opportunity to win?

This is a common sales force ploy when it is required to fulfill tasks it does not perceive in its best interest. Malicious compliance is also a term that means you get what you ask for—and no more.

The problem in this company was not bad people or even bad sales leadership. The issue was loss of confidence throughout the company, a path of least resistance created from years of revenue decline.

Skilled corporate observer Rosabeth Moss Kanter describes the effects within companies that lose their confidence after repeated attempts to reverse losses: "When losing makes people feel out of control, and when they give in to the temptations associated with defending against feeling powerless, the seeds of systemic pathologies are sown. . . . Everyone expects the worst of everyone else—and then acts to make those expectations come true. Self-confidence, confidence in one another, and confidence in the system disappear."[1]

An intuitive sales leader sees how a company's loss of confidence hurts the sales effort. Kanter says powerlessness to turn a company around produces actions that are taken to preserve control and power. Of course, their actions actually lessen it.

Departmental silos and adversarial tactics at this firm sprang from powerlessness, and department managers attempted to protect management domains. They focused on activities and results where they had relatively more control. They lost confidence in larger efforts to save the company. They did what Kanter predicted they would do. Reinforcement came from the CEO who rewarded achievement for departmental metrics, not for critically needed sales revenue. The path of least resistance was clear.

Given then a firm with managers rewarded for their defensive results, why would any of them take risks to help sales? In fact, it was in their own perceived best interest not to help sales. Thus, lacking companywide integration, sales performance suffered, morale declined further, and departmental efforts become even more parochial. It was a terrific time and place to play Monkey-in-the-Middle.

Certainly, this toxic environment was a classic Hindenburg Omen for the new CSO and all his people. Here again we see the power of context, of circumstances. At one time, most of those managers were star performers on winning teams. Now, constraints of their current environment drive their behavior within it. Hence, the turnaround solution for this company with a sales culture of losing is almost certainly not to fire the CSO.

Successful CSOs carefully assess new opportunities to learn why a predecessor "didn't work out." They determine a company's sales culture before accepting a new job. They check out the CEO's relationship with sales as well as the extent of the firm's integration behind the sales effort.

Monitoring and Supervision

Where would you look for clues about the competence of the previous sales management régime? People are rightly sensitive about how management trusts them and respects their competence. A good proxy for this sentiment is often found by learning how management monitors and supervises sales. Do measurement and control systems focus on managing behaviors, or do they focus more on managing results? Is the answer appropriate for the company's go-to-market strategy?

As a guideline, a sales organization that requires little monitoring and supervision probably understands and executes activities required to achieve results assigned to it. This company focuses on results.

What if you discover the opposite? For instance, if the focus is on behaviors and the level of supervision required is high, this may indicate a low level of skills and commitment in the sales organization. Then again, it may be perfectly appropriate for the mission. One of our telemarketing groups had a metric of "25 before nine." The goal was 25 dials before 9 AM in order to get the group limbered up for its morning meeting. Again, context is everything.

An inappropriate match of behavior management to the sales task can indicate low trust in sales and even lower self-confidence of management. Many of us have suffered under such régimes, and if we did, we may have suffered silently or headed for the exit. Whatever we did, we learned an important lesson about management. Attempts to control or measure a salesperson's every move are folly. Where can you sniff out clues about such practices? Highly talented sales reps chafe under such treatment, and this should be reflected in the company's sales high turnover metrics.

You know well that nothing is black or white. High turnover could also stem from a new compensation program. Information gives you the ability to raise important questions to ask during your discussions with the CEO. Good questions will also help you better discern the understanding and commitment of your new CEO toward the sales program you will be managing.

Even in a winning sales environment, things go wrong. Sometimes the explanation is chance or some random cause. You could lose days of production because of a freak snowstorm. At other times, the cause of a problem is simple human error. Over the past decade, researchers have explained that some human error and misjudgment is quite predictable. In the next section, we will see how the everyday sales environment affects decisions made by reps in the field. By understanding how circumstances such as uncertainty influence judgment, we can train our people to be conscious of them. At the very least, our own familiarity with sources of influence will make us wiser, more anticipative managers.

Why Good Salespeople Make Bad Decisions

My style of deal making is quite simple and straightforward. I just keep pushing and pushing and pushing to get what I'm after.

DONALD TRUMP

The 2002 Nobel Prize for economics was the first to recognize the fascinating work about the strange choices we make under uncertainty when money is involved. We do strange things, but now at least we know why. Professor Daniel Kahneman, one of two winners, explained the behavioral oddity of why we drive 20 minutes to save $5 on a $15 calculator, but won't make the same trip to buy a $125 jacket for $120, even though each action would produce exactly the same $5 savings.

As I researched work by Kahneman and others, I realized that this fascinating science of decision economics explains many poor decisions we observe in field sales. Why, for example, do sales reps continually chew up resources in low-probability sales? I found some fascinating answers.

Hold 'Em or Fold 'Em

Sales representatives make choices constantly. The best sales reps learn from their experiences and develop sales intuition that improves their success in future deals. Novices and reps who do not learn from their experience are regularly surprised when they lose deals, even those poorly qualified in the first place. In those cases, a pro would have seen familiar cautionary patterns and moved on to an opportunity with a better probability of success. Professional field sales reps "know when to hold 'em and when to fold 'em."

What is it about the high drama of the large, low-probability sale that can blind sales reps and even their managers? I observed an account team on a large deal that was oblivious to clear signs that the fix was in for another vendor. The team was being shopped for price so the buyer might complete his due diligence by comparing several prices before doing what he had planned to do anyway—give the order to his preferred vendor.

These were the facts: A Fortune 100 high-tech firm, with $100 million in services support for infrastructure and call centers, was looking to outsource everything. Scott, the sales representative, had called on the firm for more than a year. One day he received a surprise call inviting him to be one of four bidders on the request for proposal (RFP), provided he could present it within fourteen days.

He gained an extension to twenty-one days and engaged his company in a major resource commitment to meet the challenging deadline. During the weeks that followed, it became increasingly obvious that the company was being shopped. Yet, the sales team persisted and, of course, lost the bid. Using studies by Kahneman and others, we can see how this happened.

The Trigger Is Pulled

A common first misstep toward a bad decision, according to Robert Cialdini in his book *Influence* (2001), is the tendency to be triggered into action by a single feature of a situation. As a shorthand way to handle complex issues, we replay internal tapes that guide us based upon on what we've done historically in similar circumstances.

Reps who are true professionals circuit-break that tendency, first taking in all the details of a situation, and only then looking for similar shapes and patterns in their experience. They flag whatever appears out of the ordinary, according to cognitive psychologist Gary A. Klein.[2] Then, they work forward to confirm or disconfirm their intuition about the deal.

The less perceptive sales rep tends to work backward from his or her goal. Scott saw this deal as the "opportunity to get a $100-million piece of business at a Fortune 100 firm with a decision in three weeks." Then he began to address individual details without a clear view of the overarching shapes and patterns involved.

These two approaches of the novice and pro are like the intern and experienced physician diagnosing a complex case. The intern's tendency is to identify and treat individual symptoms, while the experienced doctor identifies that the symptoms fit an overall pattern of a disease, which he treats holistically.

"We all think alike, no one thinks very much," wrote columnist Walter Lippmann. This is an apt description of the chaos back at Scott's company. With little time and such a large opportunity, everyone's adrenaline was flowing. It was November. No one seriously calculated the odds of winning, since this order was the only remaining hope to achieve the year's sales target anyway. The politically correct question became, "What do we need to do to get the business?" The never-articulated question was, "Do we really have any chance at all?"

Overconfidence

Then, a human behavior principle that makes no scientific sense at all clicked into operation, the principle of overconfidence. Once we are committed to something, especially publicly, our commitment grows and we act with great consistency to prove it. For example, even though there is no change in anything, people feel more confident their horse will win after they place their bet than before. We don't even have to bet to be overconfident. It is in our nature to be predictably overconfident even in experiments that warned and paid participants to beware of this, according to consultants and professors J. Edward Russo and Paul J. H. Shoemaker.[3] Scott's team was no exception.

The Power of Reciprocity

The rule of reciprocity is a powerful one, demanding that if someone provides us something, we have an obligation to repay the gesture in kind. Author Cialdini reports that the principle is so strong, we feel compelled to comply even if we dislike the person. As Ralph Waldo Emerson said, "Pay every debt as if God wrote the bill."

A university professor demonstrated the power of reciprocity with a simple experiment. He sent a slew of Christmas cards to people who had never heard of him. He got stacks back and no one even asked who he was. Scott came under the rule of reciprocity here, and it took him another step down the road to compliance by providing a bid for a low-odds deal.

The prospect knew or should have known that no vendor could provide a well-considered bid in two weeks. So, when Scott asked for a week's extension, it was magnanimously granted. You give a little, you get a little. If the earlier deadline were impossible, the new one was nearly so, but now Scott felt obligated to comply. Scott himself initiated the deadline extension, a feather in his cap back at headquarters and now, a debt to repay.

Consistency

Looking consistent is a critical attribute for business success. Inconsistency gives off bad signals, such as not thinking something through or displaying poor judgment, crimes that can diminish the luster of a promising career. Defending one's position, even if it begins to look foolish, can become justified by the need to appear consistent. And so it was for our rep in this selling situation.

Scott told the fifteen-member support team he thought they had a good chance to win the deal. With that confidence, the team had conference calls almost daily and some members focused exclusively on details of the RFP at the expense of other projects. Though questions arose, Scott's public confidence grew like the bettor who placed his paycheck on his favorite horse.

Trust in Authority

Scott's contact was the department manager, who convinced Scott that he alone would make the decision, which "will be rubber stamped." In presenting himself as the authority in the decision, the contact appealed to the rep's sense of trust in authority. After all, most of us have learned that working along with authority is usually a successful way to gain rewards. Working against authority has never panned out as well.

What Scott failed to rationally consider is: Would a $100-million sale be a single individual's decision? The greater the risk and dollars involved, the larger number of people involved in a decision. There is usually a perfect correlation between risk and complexity of the sale.

Emotional Intelligence

Emotional intelligence includes the ability to read others accurately. Scott was emotionally involved in this "deal of a lifetime," but not reading the situation or the players shrewdly. Too late, he learned his competitor was well positioned with the company president. They were former colleagues who still had lunch together occasionally.

Given this relationship, it is highly unlikely this bid opportunity is on a level playing field. In that sobering moment Scott realized his contact lied to him. It was time for Scott to ask his CEO to become involved in the deal. A savvy rep and hands-on manager would know that $100-million decisions are always reviewed and influenced by a host of executives. Yet they held their own senior executives in reserve until it was too late.

Sunk Costs

Senior managers know that when they get a call for help so late, the deal is in flames and that they are looked to as the great firefighters. Even though the rep and his team know the deal is in trouble, they will be in bigger trouble if the loss occurs without pulling out all the stops and inviting the CEO into the sales process. Then, so the thinking goes, he shares in the defeat and can't be as critical of the account team. Though unspoken, everyone understands what is happening here, and they execute the drill anyway. It would be worse if the CEO were surprised and not asked to help.

Scott's CEO called the other CEO and, of course, received assurance that Scott's proposal was receiving a close examination. Furthermore, from what he had heard, the team had a fair shot at winning the business.

The day of the big presentation came, and Scott picked up two corporate vice presidents who flew in from headquarters. Counting them, technical specialists and others, the account team of ten arrived to battle for the mega-sale. None of them guessed that the presentation meeting would become a nightmare.

Scott's contact had not given him the courtesy of a "heads up." Their competitors had presented two days earlier. Scott's contact sheepishly told the team that the criteria for the bid had completely changed and the proposal would have to be redone. There would be no presentation that day. The contact had some "good news" for them, however. He had the temerity to tell them of their selection as one of two companies to bid on a new RFP.

There were several choices now available to the team. Behind "Door #1" was a wild card to tell the prospect exactly what they thought of the charade, and then stoically depart. They might have chosen "Door #2" and been nearly as direct at calling the game for what it was AND agreeing to rebid if they received a raft of concessions that would make it worth their while. "Door #3" permitted them to return to headquarters and bid on the new specs.

Psychologists tell us we have an irrational tendency to stay with an earlier decision when we are heavily invested in it—even when it is obviously wrong. We are reluctant to abandon such a commitment before seeing it through. This is the "sunk cost" fallacy. In short, there is a compulsion to "pour good money after bad."

The team settled for Door #3, unable to resist the temptation to take the final few steps to completion of the process. With the contest whittled down to two players, they anted up to play the last round.

Emotion

There was also a fear factor. They felt trapped between the Scylla of informing their CEO that they were pulling out of the deal with only one competitor to beat and the Charybdis of pouring even more resources into an improbable cause.

It is human nature when making decisions in uncertainty to pay more attention to the bad side of the situation in order to avoid it. Scientists tell us we fret more about a certain loss rather than risk a similar gain. Scott realized that he had a 100% probability of a painful loss review with the CEO if he threw in the towel at this point. He calculated a 30% chance of winning the deal. The team went for the 30% chance, at least forestalling the 100% probability of pain.

Decision Regret

What's more, by continuing in the game for the last round, the team also escaped the nagging cousin of "sunk costs" called "decision regret." Psychologists describe decision regret as focusing on what you might have had, if only you had stayed to play the game. This was a $100-million game and, hey, you can't win if you don't play. They agreed to roll the dice again and to submit another proposal.

Another month elapsed and more resources became consumed. Then, surprise, the award went to the competitor. Surprise again: The customer asked if Scott's team would stand at the ready should negotiations fail with the winner for a suitable contract.

The Post Mortem

There was a time when many sales managers would applaud the likes of Scott, who was pushing all the way through, playing to the end, never looking back. They didn't want their sales reps to ever let go.

Times have changed. The expense of taking a complex sale through the entire sales cycle can be astounding—into the tens or hundreds of thousands of dollars. Absent a strategic reason to bid, given costs this high, and win-likelihood so low, these deals are not affordable luxuries. How can you prevent such folly in your own organization?

First, the most successful sales managers see current reality as it is. They do not varnish the facts, and they avoid being seduced or enchanted. They ask disconfirming questions to test the "facts."

- "Have we ever seen a $100-million decision made by a guy this far down in the organization?"
- "They're telling you that there are no behind-the-scenes politics going on with a deal this size?"
- "Never having done a dollar's worth of business with this company, are they likely to flip us this bid on three weeks' work?"

The field must know where you stand. What are your standards for committing company resources? The most successful sales managers don't set metrics for funnel activity that force reps to work on poor prospects simply to meet a metric for new prospects. That's the foolish old game of asking for A (lots of prospects) while you hope for B (good prospects). In your training, walk the reps through an exercise to calculate the cost of bidding on an RFP. Ask if it were their own funds, say the $15,000 cost of a bid, would they invest given the odds, customer reputation, and parameters of the deal? What is your own standard for walking away from a deal? Shouldn't your reps know what it is so that they can adopt it, too?

Here are more ways reps can make better decisions:

- Run a training session where reps discuss and review the influence areas in a sales cycle. We have received good feedback from sessions like this. There are many "Ah-has."
- Make role playing a part of this training because it will help the learning stick. Some Machiavellian customers will spring to mind as they recall situations where these influence techniques were applied to them.

- Review the section on asking tough questions in the thin-slicing chapter. Instead of asking what you hope to confirm, ask the reps where they see red flags. Then get answers.

As difficult as it seems, walking away from sunk costs may be the smart strategy for some deals when it becomes clear that you were simply being shopped for a price to compare to the prospect's preferred vendor. I rarely see this happen, and yet it is the logical decision to stop the flow of good money after bad.

I pulled my sales team out of a major hospital bid where it seemed foolish to continue the pursuit. We had footed the expense of two first-class field trips and countless sales hours. The account was prestigious and highly visible. There was some political risk for all of us. I met with our contact and gave him the unexpected news that we were withdrawing our bid. He was surprised. With nothing more to lose we left him with much valuable advice to aid his task—along with some caveats about our chief competitor. Then we moved on and went after deals we could win.

He surprised us a month later. He called to ask us, now his preferred winner, back into the contest. Our honest predictions had come to pass. He also had had to answer some tough questions about why we had left the contest. Overall, it was a nice win, but I cannot recommend this as a predictable tactic!

Recommendations

- Test the offer. There are flags that reps should spot along the sales cycle.

- Expand contacts. A relationship based upon a single contact is unquestionably shaky. A contact person is more likely to be forthright if he knows your rep is relating to others in the company.

- Give the buyer an assignment. The sale is only moving forward when the buyer commits to action. Just because your rep is working like a dog does not mean anything relative to the outcome of the bid. We know of a successful senior sales executive who tests his prospects by assigning them work to do. If the prospect does not produce the promised information at their next meeting, he halts his effort.

- Watch rep activity for balance. Reps, particularly newer ones, can get so distracted by opportunities like this one that they drop the rest of their pipeline. Successful sales leaders ensure that they develop other business. The odds of winning such large deals are long. Smart sales managers know this and cover their objectives by winning enough smaller deals.

- Avoid enchantment. Be aware yourself of influences that tend to create an automatic response in your reps. Teach them to institute an internal circuit breaker before falling under the spell. Demonstrate it yourself.

- Avoid overconfidence. Reps are optimistic. Realistically calibrate their confidence level by pointing out uncertainties. We are usually overconfident about what we think we know.

CHAPTER 4

Sales Control and Policies

If you want to make enemies, try to change something.

WOODROW WILSON

Sales Controls

Controls are the company's method of directing and measuring sales activity across the entire organization. Typical sales controls include quota assignments, compensation, expense budgets, activity or funnel reporting, gift policy, rules, forecasting, travel and entertainment reporting and policies, car policy, territory, account selection, and training programs. Sales controls also include derivative metrics such as call activity, close ratio, turnover, and quota performance. Without controls and policies, sales managers would spend unproductive time making individual decisions that are easily codified by controls and policies.

Without controls, chaos would reign. Unfortunately, controls that are unenlightened, inconsistent, or misdirected can also lead to chaos. In the following case, observe how a well-intended compensation plan change boomeranged into a disaster.

Second-Level Consequences

Sales reps are extraordinarily aware when it comes to their compensation plans. They do what they are paid to do, and little more. Even when an unpaid activity is of high value to the company, sales reps are reluctant helpers. If you want to drive behavior, write the appropriate carrot into their compensation plan. That sounds easy enough.

Unfortunately, it is not. Managers often fail to think through the consequences of new decisions. Nobel Prize winner Tversky terms this "nonconsequentialist reasoning." He concludes that we tend to follow a path of least resistance. It's more work to look ahead, and easier to look back. Yet, as the next illustration demonstrates, the most successful sales managers should always push themselves to consider the second-level consequences of their decisions.

My assignment was to coach a new CSO whose sales steadily trended down. I noted that the company's standard contract had a provision for one-, two-, or three-year agreements just by checking a box. According to the marketing staff, almost all the contracts were for one year. Further, marketing believed that the disinterest in longer-term contracts portended a swift decline in the company's offering.

This view clashed with other research that showed the company's offering as fairly priced and well supported. I discovered a well-intended compensation plan change that explained everything. The CEO had made a comp plan change that moved a commission from one product to another. The CEO eliminated compensation on the second and third year's sales. He moved the commission funds to emphasize a new product important for the company's future. He intended that sales would not lose commissions. They would just be shifted in order to change behavior. He knew that new products sell faster when they have extra incentive, i.e., he was looking back to his experience. He had not looked forward to the impact on the current product.

In his view, the sales effort was already well rewarded for the first year of a new service contract. All that was required to extend the sale to two or three years was a check mark in a box on the contract. In his view, no more effort was required for a multiyear contract, so why pay for it.

Almost immediately, the company had a sharp drop in multiyear service contracts. The sales force regarded the compensation change negatively. It considered these commissions as taken away rather than simply shifted. The CEO had a logically defensible position, and so did the sales force.

They felt it was unfair to strip a commission because someone believed the sale was too easy. After all, just getting the contract signed in the first place required lot of effort. Furthermore, they reasoned that the company would receive revenue for years two and three of a contract without any compensation expense. Difficulty of the sale notwithstanding, the revenue dollars were still the same. They felt the company was unfairly receiving a benefit they provided and taking away one that they deserved.

Multiyear sales at the same commission as single-year sales would have helped the company. Now there was no incentive to sign them—even if the sale were relatively easier.

Actually, the reverse was true. There was now an incentive NOT to get two- and three-year contracts. Reps realized they would get a full commission when they resold the service next year. There were even more unintended consequences.

As multiyear sales of contracts continued to drop, more accounts were lost to competitors. The CEO's change and sales' response put their customers into a mode of constant shopping for renewal options. To put it differently, saving a few bucks on commissions cost the company hundreds of thousands of dollars in lost accounts to competitors.

Of course, there was another unintended consequence. Instead of stimulating sales of the new product, the reps sold less of it. This was due to the power of the path of least resistance. It is easier to resell an old customer than create a new one.

Predictably, when renewal time came, the rep would invest his time to re-sign his existing account for another year. To summarize, the company added fewer new accounts and never received the expected push for the new product line.

When the CEO realized the full implication of what he had done, he restored full commission for each additional year of service signed at the time of the contract. Again, context turns out to be everything. The minute the structure was changed, the path of least resistance changed also. The sales force exhibited predictable behavior.

Moral: Think beyond the first-stage implication of every change. Even seemingly small changes can have significant, unintended consequences on revenue, morale, and market share.

There are many factors that make a sales culture successful or not. These include training, MBOs, territory sizes, ability to meet targets, and others already mentioned. The compensation plan is the most important of them all. Sales does what it is paid to do.

Many CEOs are unfamiliar with how sales compensation works. As in the example above, the CEO may think it is obvious that a sales rep would rationally do what is best for the company. However, as the case illustrates, do not count on it.

The "Art" of Forecasting

Books have been written on the science of forecasting, but anyone in the real world of sales knows that forecasting is no science at all. Rather, it's more like an art—subjective and inexact. Why then do monthly floggings continue until forecasting improves? Let's start at the top.

CEOs Live by Numbers

Achieving metrics drives CEO earnings. So, they think in metrics and talk of metrics. They got to where they are because they made their numbers. Remember that more of today's CEOs come from engineering than any other discipline. By experience, they believe numbers can describe nearly everything, that numbers can characterize all activity and make it binary. Any number—such as a sales forecast—is either hit or missed. A contract is signed or it isn't. However, selling and forecasting sales are not simple binary operations. What makes sales different from other corporate functions?

Apples and Oranges

When a CEO was, say, VP of Operations, he could accurately forecast many metrics. He had personal control over many of them and, therefore, the power to control a measure of forecasting precision. By not filling a personnel position, for example, expenses would decrease predictably. As VP of Finance, he could be an expert cash manager by not paying or prepaying bills. In these examples, actions are causal of results. With causal control over operations, the VPs demonstrated the "science" of accurate forecasting. So, your boss and colleagues wonder: Why can't sales managers demonstrate this science?

Shades of Gray

To be a science, a body of knowledge must demonstrate facts or truths. However, facts and truths are difficult to come by in sales. Most situations are shades of gray. The same "facts" may produce different outcomes.

For instance, the CFO yields to sales' request for a price cut and wants to know, "What price do you need to win the deal?" In this case, the discount wins the sale. Another manager gets the same discount only to lose his sale. A sales manager understands immediately why this happens, while many CFOs shake their heads in bewilderment. In truth, the CFO is unaware of how much he doesn't know about sales. Unfortunately, this doesn't restrain him from misperceiving the competence of the sales department.

Sales knows of the many nonprice variables that enter into a sale. Variables vary often unpredictably. A sudden spending may delay a certain sale. This is why sales forecasts are not governed by consistently repeatable principles and therefore not a science. Sales forecasts are really an art, more the result of intuition, clairvoyance, and probability.

Some 350 years ago, the French mathematician Pascal explained this difference in his famous *Pensées*. There are, he said, differences between scientific and intuitive matters. Scientific matters are those in which reasonable men would come to the same conclusion by applying the facts. There are 90° in a right triangle; therefore, anyone can spot the error of a claim that there are 89°. This is science because the nature of the matter is perfectly definite once you collect the relevant information.

The Realm of Probability

Whether a sale will close is not a perfectly definite idea. In a pending sale, the amount of information that exists to describe the situation is nearly infinite. Which information is relevant? Are there unknown factors that will be more relevant? A sale cannot be described with the precision of a right triangle. It can only be described as a probability.

Sales Forecasting Is Intuitive

Describing a pending sale is more akin to describing other indefinite terms such as "love"! With similar difficulty to providing the definition of "love," the closing date of a sale leaves plenty of room for variation from thoughtful observers. Pascal would call these situations matters of intuition or "finesse." In these matters, as opposed to scientific ones, there is sometimes such a large body of information to be digested that the task becomes increasingly complex because of variables that cannot be assigned values and solved like an equation. How do we even know that we have collected all or at least enough information upon which to base a decision? In other words, how can we know what we don't know?

Sales Representatives Have Unequal Skills

There is a further complication in forecasting accurately. In interpreting the set of facts in a sales situation, not every sales representative has the same experience and discernment to draw the same conclusions. Thus, even with all the facts, there is wide variation due to interpretation. Even experts can disagree on the consequences of the same set of facts. Of course, it depends upon your definition of "all"!

Who Is Really in Charge of the Sale?

Unlike the examples in finance and operations above where an executive had control over variables, sales may influence, but not control the ultimate variable. In sales it is the customer who holds the power to determine when a sale will close, not the salesperson. Therefore, while the sales force pushes for decisions in a timely manner, complex internal customer relationships, shifting politics, competitive wildcards, last-minute demands, and more may conspire against the most eloquent urgings of the sales representative upon his prospect.

In a company with large volumes of sales orders, the law of large numbers smooths out the good guesses and the bad. It is a scientific law that the more numbers calculated, the closer the result approaches its true value. The forecasting process is most nerve-wracking where your desired company results are skewed by a relatively few substantial sales. Every sale becomes high profile because even a single customer delay can destroy your sales forecast.

Probability: The Forecast Is Wrong

The consensus among sales executives I asked is that in a given month, only one in four deals—25%—forecast by the sales force will actually close. That is why most executives filter the field forecast through their first-line managers, or apply their own experience factor, or divide by π before they send the forecast to the CEO.

While you may be in the statistical ballpark for the total monthly number, unfortunately, for any particular deal that the boss asks about, the odds are still against you. Table 4.1 shows why. There are just too many variables for a sales rep to forecast with dead-on accuracy in a single account. Let us look at the permutations involved in predicting that a particular deal will close this month.

As Table 4.1 shows, the rep can be right that the deal will close or right that it will not close. If this happened often enough, there would be no need for this chapter on forecasting! However, if her intuition is off, she can be wrong about a deal closing or wrong that a deal that she thought would not close will close.

The wildcard is always the customer, who can still sign or not sign regardless of whether the rep read the situation correctly.

Pascal was right. Some matters are easily determined to be right or wrong, yes or no. Sales forecasting is not one of them!

Nevertheless, Forecasting Is Essential

The difficulty of forecasting not withstanding, how do you satisfy your CEO and colleagues who require one? As we noted, the difficulty and importance vary by your individual context. Here are some ideas from successful managers in a variety of environments.

- Educate your CEO and colleagues about the specific difficulties that present themselves. With thought you can make a factual case describing the particular factors for your environment. Explain how the set of variables involved adds difficulty to the sales forecasting equation.

- Some CSOs sit down with their most vocal or critical colleagues to negotiate a truce from public criticism. They explain the issues described above. Then they lay out alternatives to address the particular criticisms. For example, would the colleague prefer quarterly forecasts? Then listen and negotiate an agreement that works for both of you.

- Developing agreement like this can have the effect of turning an enemy into an ally. Particularly if the criticism of your forecasting has become public, such as in staff meetings, you can lower the heat by announcing the new approach agreed upon.

TABLE 4.1 Probability in Forecasts

Three Forecasting Variables			
1. The rep has all information required for an informed forecast.*	2. The rep interprets the information and forecasts correctly based upon it.*	3. The customer acts as the rep predicts.*	The Statistical Probability of Forecasting Correctly
Combinations of the Variables*			
Yes	Yes	Yes	100%
Yes	Yes	No	12.5%
Yes	No	No	12.5%
Yes	No	Yes	12.5%
No	No	No	12.5%
No	No	Yes	12.5%
No	Yes	Yes	12.5%
No	Yes	No	12.5%

*There are eight (2^3) possible combinations. Assume 50% probability for each variable, e.g., the rep may or may not have all the required information for an informed forecast; the rep may have the information, but misinterpret it, etc.

- With large account responsibility, quarterly or semi-annual forecasting can even out extreme monthly vicissitudes.

- A successful international manager advises having enough flexibility in your pipeline to add in or take out pending sales in order to smooth out a forecast if a large pending sale suddenly goes awry.

- Be realistic. Don't apply more time or resources for the forecasting task beyond the point of diminishing returns. Instead, devote executive resources to actual customer sales and retention.

- Have a Top Ten list of sales to be personally involved in. You will always know what's really happening in the key accounts.

- One Sales Vice President, now a CEO, maintains a practice he found effective on his way to the top. In addition to his longer term participation in his Top Ten accounts, he watched his "Hot Five." These were the top five hottest situations with short-term decision horizons. This personal account team level involvement helped him forecast accurately.

- Study carefully your sales trends to generate a statistically likely forecast, or . . .

- Develop a list of objective criteria that any potential sale must satisfy before it can be forecast. For example, an account may not be forecast until your contract been approved by the customer's legal department. This is a highly effective method to improve forecasts. It adds objectivity and can help you hammer out agreements with critical colleagues.

- Understand the quality of your product/market match. No one is better situated than you to use market and competitive trends to keep your company viable. This means spotting opportunities for innovation and creative business relationships.

- Become well educated on your competition. Find out why they win and lose sales. Influence your customers and internal colleagues with valuable intelligence. Tell your colleagues what you see as longer-term trends.

- Finally, stay in constant contact with your top customers. Create close relationships you can use to influence other sales, or to save you when your business with their company is in jeopardy. The degree to which you are intimately knowledgeable of your customer's business and their customers' needs is the measure of the value you bring as a collaborative partner.

Thin-Slicing, a Productivity Tool

In his best-selling book on human cognition, *Blink,*[1] author Malcolm Gladwell introduces readers to a phrase from the world of psychology: "the power of thin-slicing." In the book, Gladwell offers many fascinating examples of people making sense of situations based on the thinnest slice of experience—overhearing as little as one or two seconds of a conversation, for example.

Cook County Hospital (CCH) is a wonderful example of identifying just the right amount of information by thin-slicing. At CCH, the approach saved lives and resources. Just ahead, you will see how sales managers can use this same technique to win more bids and save resources.

In financial crisis, CCH sought to cut costs for its ER's most costly service—diagnosing heart attacks. A heart attack is not an easy thing to diagnose, and no one wants to send a victim home who is actually experiencing one. Therefore, in exercising due care, ER doctors routinely ordered many tests that in retrospect were unnecessary—and expensive.

CCH had no standard best practice to diagnose an actual heart attack in progress. There were as many ways to diagnose heart attacks as there were physicians. The administration believed that it could reduce costs and deliver good care if it could identify the best indicators of a probable heart attack and have every physician use them. The question was, "How much information was enough?"

They implemented the findings of a study demonstrating that just four relatively easily determined pieces of information, such as blood pressure, would suffice. CCH had its staff implement the practice. The first step was a successful trial. Then CCH implemented its four-step algorithm as standard practice.

Thin-slicing has obvious applications for sales management to identify better prospects particularly from among RFPs.

Thin-Slicing RFPs

In many companies, each rep applies his own criteria to select an unsolicited RFP on which he wishes to bid. Choices are subjective and there is no agreement about even what constitutes an "unsolicited" RFP, let alone a good one. Where CCH relied upon each physician's own opinion, the default position in sales often is reliance upon the quality of the rep's own judgment. This practice can lead to the waste of resources, especially since many companies have predetermined their choice of vendor. Our study showed that in more than half of RFP requests, they are shopping you for a comparison price against their preferred vendor.

Sometimes, the rep can be drawn to bid on marginal opportunities because he has nothing better to work on. He may even bid an opportunity merely to fulfill an activity requirement or just to look busy.

Thin-slicing is an effective way to incorporate the best learning of others to the benefit of all. It helps reps at all experience levels select the best opportunities for investment of the company's resources into winning deals.

Creating Your Thin-Slicing Tool for RFPs.   Thin-slicing is not complicated. First, develop a checklist of criteria that appear to have worked in the past to identify the best opportunities. "In retrospect, what did we know or wish we had known to determine if the opportunity were real?" Make a list of all the insights you collect from your analysis and advice of your most successful producers. Then combine and narrow your list to the few best insights. Rate all RFP requests on whether they meet or do not meet your predetermined criteria. In order to receive resources to work on a project not meeting criteria, a sales manager's override is required. Then track the results of your system adjusting it when you learn something new. The steps below break out the process in more detail.

Step 1: Hard Evidence.   Gather some hard evidence and include the opinions of your best performers about characteristics of good RFP opportunities. Your list of favorable factors may include:

- The size of the deal: It is in our sweet spot.

- We can influence proposal development: We have a pre-existing relationship with this prospect.

- This is a leading-edge account: It is a strategic opportunity. This is an attractive account with enormous growth potential.

- We have a competitive advantage: Our offer is superior to the competition, or their current supplier has failed them or is unable to meet their expectations.

- We have a fair chance to win: There is a level playing field. We have access to the key players. The decision maker is personally involved. They are "switchable" from our competitor.

- The purchase is budgeted: This is not just a fishing expedition.

- We are positioned with the decision maker: We have a position of influence, not simply acquaintance.

- We helped write the RFP, the new VP selected us at his former company. We have a good solution. Our product is a great match for this opportunity.

- They want to grow: We add real value to their offer.

Step 2: Group and Combine. Now group, combine, and quantify your list. Identify the few pieces of hard evidence that allow you in retrospect to pick what you now know were the best opportunities. These become your thin-slicing criteria going forward.

Dig down to collect hard evidence: Did we have a pre-existing relationship? Was it important? What really is a relationship? Were we certain the project was budgeted? Did we have access to decision makers? Did it matter? Did we later find that someone had an inside edge? How could we have known that earlier? How many of our bids were "no decision"? Were we being shopped, euphemistically, the "designated loser"? You will begin to see some patterns.

Perhaps having a pre-existing relationship jumped out as predictor. On the laundry list above, there are several items suggesting the importance of a prior relationship. Perhaps you find that you won almost no deals without it. Thus, meeting this criterion then becomes a "must" for bidding on an opportunity.

Use "must" criteria sparingly because there are times when you ought to take strategic risks even with low odds of success. Your future success comes from developing new relationships with growing firms who are worth competing for. The trick is to carefully select these situations.

Step 3: Weighting. Next, weight your indicators relative to each other. The most important indicator will have a relative weight of three and the least important indicator a relative weight of one.

Now, clarify what an indicator means by creating a satisfaction scale to explain it. Leave as little room for interpretation as possible. Example (see Figure 4.1):

1. The Indicator in Figure 4.1 is weighted "3," of highest relative importance.

2. Note that the Attractiveness Scale provides only three possible scores 0, 5, and 10.

3. To evaluate an RFP on this indicator, the rep would simply circle the attractiveness score and multiply it by the weighting score of three.

(1) Indicator: "We have a fair chance to compete and win."	Relative Weight 3
(2) Attractiveness Scale (choose one)	
We influenced RFP, well-positioned	10
Will have access to key people	5
Competitor stronghold, not positioned	0
(3) Rating	
Points: 3 (weight) X 0 = Total 0	

FIGURE 4.1   Bidding on an RFP.

To rate this indicator for an unsolicited RFP from an account where your team is not positioned, the rep would circle zero. The overall Satisfaction Points awarded to this particular indicator is calculated in this example as "0."

If you have four key indicators and their total relative importance weighting is, say, 10 (3, 2, 3, 2), and each indicator has a potential 10 attractiveness points, a perfect opportunity would receive a score of 100. Since few opportunities will be perfect 100s, what is the minimum score for an acceptable opportunity?

Step 4: Test. Create several phantom opportunities to test your thin-slicing algorithm. Rate them to develop a feel for how many points an opportunity should score to be worthy of resources for a bid. Take your phantom candidate through each indicator and determine the minimum acceptable rating for each. Add the minimum acceptable scores and that number becomes your threshold score. Anything below the threshold should not be bid or require an override by a sales manager.

Keep records and adjust the algorithm as you learn more. Keep in mind that you're not after perfection, just a guide that gives everyone standards, access to the organization's best thinking, and allocates resources wisely.

Alternative Thin-Slicing Algorithm (Table 4.2).

Step 1. Spread 100 points (column 2) among your criteria (column 1) to reflect their importance relative to each other. To make

TABLE 4.2 Alternate RFP Bid Analysis

1. Indicator/Criteria	2. Relative Importance	3. Weighting Factor
We have a relationship with this customer.	40	4
The decision maker is involved.	20	2
We have access to key people.	20	2
We have a competitive advantage.	20	2
Total	100	10

the numbers easier to work with, divide each weighting number by 10. This becomes a weighting factor (column 3).

Step 5: Attributes (Table 4.3). Define desirable (column 2) and undesirable (column 3) attributes the reps will use to award their satisfaction points.

Step 6: Quantify the Result (Table 4.4). Simply multiply the Weighting Factor times the number of Attractiveness Points. This

TABLE 4.3 Attributes

Criteria	2. Desirable Award up to 5 points	3. Undesirable Award 0-2 points
We have a relationship with this customer. (Weight 4)	Customer account. Well positioned.	We were invited to bid and have no account positioning.
The decision maker is involved. (Weight 2)	A real deal. High likelihood of a decision. Executive has a problem and is personally involved in solving it.	Probable fishing expedition to gather information. Low confidence that this has funding or executive following.
We have access to key people. (Weight 2)	Opportunity to influence decision at multiple levels and to get information required for our bid.	Locked into single contact. Cannot influence others or gather info on full scope of opportunity.
We have a competitive advantage. (Weight 2)	We have a compelling value or product advantage as perceived by the prospect.	No compelling reason for account to change suppliers.
This is a strategic account. (Rate: Yes or No)	All competitive gear but we have a good opportunity for a toehold.	Fast-growing, desirable customer.

TABLE 4.4   Quantifying Results

Indicator	1. Relationship/ Positioning	2. D.M. Involved	3. Access Key People	4. Competitive Advantage
Weight Points	4	2	2	2
0-5 Indicator Satisfaction	3.5	1	1.5	2
Total	14	2	3	4

Summary:	*Total 23*
	Not Strategic

provides a Total Satisfaction of 23 points, which may or may not meet your threshold. The Strategic Account box acts as a flag for further discussion if the rep indicates "Yes."

Whatever process you use to rate your proposal requests, remember your goal is smarter application of your resources, not an onerous process. Once created, the thin-slicing tools should take minutes to complete. You will not achieve perfection, but every risky bid you screen out is worth real money in resources saved and re-employed on a bid that favors you. In addition, everyone develops better discernment and intuitive judgment. Over time, you can even estimate the value of your thin-slicing process by valuing resources saved and new opportunities engaged by working smarter.

Review

Always remember that no one wants his or her judgment replaced by an algorithm. Each person feels that he or she has an important perspective to consider. These conversations help keep you close to your market.

Be certain to get input from your best performers to develop evidence upon which to build your algorithm. Studies show again and again that "expert" opinion significantly increases the reliability of a tool such as this. A group of experts tends to smooth out the bias of a single expert.

Test your model by plugging in some historical cases. Would your system have worked to identify the best prospects? Would you have bid on a Cisco project when it was just starting up? Systems like this are not foolproof, which is why you ought to have an override appeal for a rep who thinks he is bidding on the next Cisco.

Debrief all RFP wins and losses to improve your model and future win ratio. Look for trends in override RFPs that may indicate sophisticated judgment of a rep or overconfidence in another.

Qualifying the Old-Fashioned Way

If you have few bid opportunities, here is a simple, old-fashioned, effective approach to improve the quality of your prospect funnel. There are no forms and no game playing.

The old softball game begins with the rep and the prospect. Notice how well each has learned to ask and listen as the other has taught him over the years:

> **REP:** "Does any vendor have an inside track?"
> **PROSPECT:** "Of course not."
> **REP:** "Is the money budgeted?"
> **PROSPECT:** "It certainly is."
> **REP:** "Who is making the decision?"
> **PROSPECT:** "Me. They will rubber stamp my decision."

Often the questioning is no more incisive than this back at the office. The rep is prepared with the answers he knows his manager wants to hear. Unfortunately, while this burlesque accomplishes its purpose of not overqualifying to scare off prospects, this qualifying filter lets almost anything through. If your people are doing this, they are wishful thinkers who will cost you resources better applied elsewhere.

Asking softball questions is another version of failed thinking called confirmation bias. We love information that confirms what we want to hear. This tendency plays into the normal overconfidence of sales managers who form perceptions too quickly. The following bullet points can help you focus on real opportunities.

- Wishful thinking and confirmation bias distort the way that we perceive and use information. As nice as it is to hear what you want to hear about a new opportunity, remember to ask some disconfirming questions to double-check yourself. What questions could you ask that, if true, would make this a questionable prospect?

- Disconfirming questions raise new issues, which may take the bloom off the rose. Ask a rep, "Would you invest $15,000 of your own cash bid on this opportunity?" You quickly see his or her confidence or lack of!

- There is a reason for everything—including why a prospect invites your company to bid on a deal. When you qualify them, prospects can be very flattering about the importance of receiving a bid from market leaders like you. Often, you need to dig deeper for the whole story. One experienced manager we interviewed recalled this personal example of hidden agendas.

  A New Jersey County School Board invited him to provide a quote for 85 new telephone systems. "What an opportunity!" he thought initially. Rather than be carried away with wishful thinking, he decided to ask some tough qualifying (disconfirming) questions to determine just how real this opportunity was. The time he invested in qualifying more deeply paid off well.

  He discovered a Machiavellian plan by the regional school authority to use him and other vendors to wrest power from local boards. Their first step was to get an attractive bid to demonstrate their ability to save tax dollars through centralized buying power. If local districts took in this Trojan horse, the trap was sprung. The telecom oversight responsibility would translate to job security for them at the cost of local autonomy. Our friend declined to bid on the 85 systems. "Winning would have been awful," he said.

  To be low bidder, he would have cut his margin. Then he would have had his next surprise. He would have learned that winning would not be an order for 85 systems. Rather, as preferred vendor he would depart for an extended road show to sell the systems one school at a time. As someone once said about being tarred and feathered, if it were not for the honor of it, I would just as soon skip the ceremony. Your own experience may tell you this is not an atypical case. All companies can become targets of internal power plays.

- Disconfirming questions are always prudent. There is little downside and enormous benefit potential just by asking. As John Stuart Mill observed, truth can only be sharpened by its collision with error.

How a Super Salesman Avoided Common Decision Traps

Our sales managers' conference invited the country's leading salesperson to tell us the reasons for his success. Bobby F. talked of the importance of planning and time management, but the part that was most profound was his discussion about prospecting.

He explained that his sales manager always provided him with the first refusal on any leads that came in. That was out of respect for his success rate and the need to help him avoid any activity that would be a time waster. When a lead interested him, he met personally with the prospect to qualify him. Bobby had worked out what he called his track.

The track was simply an explanation of how the two would agree to proceed toward determining if Bobby's product was a match for the customer's need. If the customer did not meet the criteria Bobby had established, or if he could not agree to cooperate in moving along the track that he thought he had established, then the lead would be turned back in to his sales manager, who would pass it on to another sales rep in the office.

The Lead Didn't Qualify

Now here is the key part of the story. The new salesperson receiving the lead would approach him and say, "Bobby, I just got this lead on one of your prospects. What can you tell me about him?"

"I will tell you that he did not qualify."

"But, Bobby, everybody knows how hard you qualify these people. Please tell me what you know about him."

"Again, I'll tell you that he did not qualify."

The difference between his success and the lack of success for others boiled down to whether a prospect qualified for his time and effort. After all, he said all he had to give was his time, and it made no sense to waste it upon a poor prospect.

The question arises, then, Why would another rep choose to pursue a prospect that the top salesperson in the country perceived as not qualifying?

To answer this critical question we can look to work by Daniel Kahneman as mentioned by and Shoemaker, Russo, and others. It appears that about six common decision traps might entice the less experienced sales rep to take on this unqualified account.

The *endowment theory* observes that we tend to value something in our own possession more highly than another possession of the same value in the hands of another. I saw this demonstrated in a sales management class at Columbia University. The instructor gave mugs and T-shirts of equivalent monetary value to sales managers in the class. They were told that both items were equivalent in value; T-shirts were equivalent to the mugs. The question was asked how many were willing to trade even for a gift in possession of another manager. The answer was very few people. The reason was that once each had possession of his or her own gift, psychologically it assumed greater value than the gift of another.

The rookie salesman in our example felt a similar ownership of the lead given him by the sales manager. He owned it, and therefore it must have more value than Bobby perceived to have. In fact, the lead would usually turn out to have a negative value because of the time and effort wasted confirming Bobby's evaluation.

Bobby carefully avoided the psychological principle of *sunk cost*. He invested in the time to prepare for the customer call and to make the call itself without being reluctant to fold his hand and toss the lead back to the sales manager. Kahnemann tells us that most of us are reluctant to admit our losses—in this case the time invested in qualifying the account. Typically, we somehow feel that any cost invested into the customer is a reasonable basis to continue the given the investment that we have already made.

The less experienced sales rep was often unable to avoid the *status quo effect*. This decision trap encourages us psychologically to stay the course of a prior decision, even when an impartial observer could judge that the initial decision was in error.

If the sales rep who decided to pursue the unqualified lead simply stopped to think about *simple probability,* he would have also returned to lead to the sales manager. This is a common error we make in tending to overvalue low-probability situations. Perhaps this is a function of perceiving that the lead from management may be of some value (the endowment effect); however, a salesperson playing the odds would note that an account Bobby considered unqualified would be a low-probability account. By pursuing it, he was overvaluing a low-probability situation.

There is also the *regret fallacy,* which means that we will not gain some potential good result if we never follow a situation through to its denouement. It's common with many of us who hear all the "if only" stories about colossal gains foregone by fearing to make the attempt.

Finally, Bobby's story of prospecting shows an additional talent he has that is lacking in his less experienced peers. That talent is *mental simulation.* It is affiliated with intuition and allows Bobby to quickly think through the steps ahead in the potential prospect relationship to identify high-probability disconnects in the future given the feedback he received from the prospect on his initial call.

Table 4.5 compares the dramatic extremes between a highly experienced and an inexperienced salesperson in avoiding decision traps to make a fundamentally critical decision, namely where to invest limited time.

TABLE 4.5 Comparing Experience

Decision Trap	Bobby	Less Experienced Salesperson
Endowment effect	Avoided the trap	Susceptible
Sunk cost fallacy	Avoided the trap	Susceptible
Status quo effect	Avoided the trap	Susceptible
Overvaluing probability	Avoided the trap	Susceptible
Regret	Avoided the trap	Susceptible
Mental simulation	Avoided the trap	Susceptible

CHAPTER 5

Channels

The surest way for an executive to kill himself is to refuse to learn how and when and to whom to delegate.

J. C. PENNEY

The aim of a marketing alliance is to position your company as an attractive supplier of what a buyer is looking for. CEOs and CSOs may create alliances that look great and press-worthy from a high level, but that may not help the field.

Depending upon their fit for your market, go-to-market partners win or kill deals. A partner offering, dynamite in a large enterprise bid, may be cost ineffective in SME (small and medium enterprise) markets. By partnering on an SME deal, the partner's pricing may put your sales organization at a disadvantage. The partner may have a great reputation in his market, but what's important is his effectiveness for your customers.

Consider the second-level consequences of every alliance. That is, consider how the relationship will work in practice. One of my clients negotiated an alliance with EDS. At first blush, it seemed like a powerful relationship given EDS's reputation and humongous size. Unfortunately, nothing worked as hoped. This is where thinking through second-level consequences is important.

67

My client was only a speck on the radar screen of EDS teams bidding for new sales. When this became apparent, the client sales managers made selling initiatives at EDS branch offices. Unfortunately, EDS branch managers rarely had time for them, and most were unaware of the intercompany alliance.

My client CSO learned some valuable lessons. The CEO had negotiated the alliance and then dropped it into his lap. Next time he would:

- Ask his CEO to stay involved until the details were agreed.
- Ask his CEO to host another meeting to introduce the CSO and gain agreement on implementation and operational details.
- Get agreement from his CEO and EDS on objectives.
- Had his own EDS contact assigned and committed to implement the agreement.
- Gain agreement for a future session to review progress toward objectives.

Role of Partners

Good partners help you get to market sooner, selling solutions that are more complete and help to reduce the risk of entering new markets. They bring skills you do not have and contacts you may never develop. In the new market, you may not have the time or investment money to add essential technical personnel to your staff. Savvy partners can this forestall or save altogether an investment in resources, allow you to get to know the market much more quickly, significantly shorten the sales cycle, and, last but not least, improve your win rate by adding value you cannot.

Carefully think potential partnerships through their second-level consequences. It's important to understand how potential partnerships can help or hurt the sales effort of your organization.

One start-up CEO reported that terms and commissions of partner relationships vary "wildly." Therefore, it can be advantageous to have several alliances with differing offers so that your field organization can select the best among them for a custom solution and a better win-rate.

Alliances Can Position You

Prospecting is tough business. Many of the best introductions to new opportunities come through third parties who already know the customers. In some markets is almost impossible to reach decision makers without an introduction.

At the Information Week CIO conference, I polled enough CIOs to verify that almost none believe in taking cold calls. Either they already know what they need or get so many calls that they do not have time to sort them out. One CIO reported that when he gets 135 calls (the capacity of his voice mailbox), he deletes them all. All this call avoidance by CIOs adds another layer of difficulty to the sales job in challenging competitive markets.

Yet, with a referral from someone he knows, you could probably get your call returned. Ask for introductions. It's one of the favors a good partner is glad to grant.

These less formal alliances may not accomplish your objectives as you grow and require greater coverage or decide to outsource part or all of the sales function. You may decide to create your own channel of intermediaries to go to market. Formal sales channels to resell or agency services deserve books in themselves. Many of the insights you gain here are readily applied to formal channel relationships. The next section presents another use of thin-slicing to help you avoid problems even the largest companies encounter.

Thin-Slicing in a Sales Channel

Before its acquisition, AT&T asked me to work with a group of newly appointed channel managers who had responsibility to create AT&T's first indirect sales channel for its long-distance products. All of these managers were experienced sales managers but only a few had had channel management experience. We created a complete program including an agency contract, compensation program, training, agent selection process, and more.

AT&T considered its long-distance services the company crown jewels. As such, the company was one of the last to create a sales agency program to distribute its services. At first AT&T's newly minted channel managers recruited new agents carefully. They collected pages of information on prospective agents, following it up with an on-site inspection and face-to-face interviews with the agent's senior team. The quality of the new sales agents, I knew, would be one of the key factors in the program's success. Of course, we looked for agents with good customer bases who could sell the services in the required volume. It was just as important to select agents whose go-to-market tactics preserved AT&T's brand reputation—one of the best in all the world.

The program ramped and quickly exceeded its sales objectives. Then, the executive in charge made a decision that would cost AT&T and its sales agents millions of dollars. To compensate for a projected shortfall from direct sales, he mandated a sudden arbitrary quota increase for the indirect channel. AT&T's channel managers scrambled to add new agents to carry the quota. In their haste, they took shortcuts in the recruitment and selection process. They no longer visited every prospective partner, now confident that the questionnaire and telephone interview provided sufficient information for their decisions.

Even with good selections, agents normally required six months before producing consistently. With the poor agents now entering the program, that ramp-up could extend indefinitely. As results failed to meet new expectations, the channel recruiters became more stressed, took more shortcuts, and unfortunately recruited more incompetent agents.

Agents were added based on a telephone conversation and a mailed application. In yet another shortcut, regional managers were no longer required to approve applications before headquarters activated their contracts.

With the quality standards for admission to the program dropping, it was not long before the channel management team faced another problem. The direct sales force started to wail about the tactics of their indirect channel brethren. They were promised that the channel would target smaller customers, leaving the major accounts to the direct sales force. This did nothing to stop many agents from selling services into even the largest accounts where they had established relationships. In the short term, poaching the direct team accounts improved the channel results by bringing in larger sales.

Now, the new channel management team faced battles on two fronts. They were behind quota, and they had alienated the direct sales organization. They could not anticipate the impact of this second strategic blunder. The direct sales organization is always better positioned with top managers at headquarters. It understands headquarters politics and knows which doors to knock on to create political pressure for its cause.

The pressure began to build as headquarters executives pressured the channel management team to sell within its own segments. Had the channel managers effectively done so, they would have alienated their best channel members and reduced their own results.

Six months later, channel management's poor decisions came back to haunt them. By year-end, they had signed on 500 sales agents. Even so, results were below objectives. Complaints from the direct organization reached a crescendo. On a dark day for the channel team and its new agents, AT&T suspended the program. Ultimately, most of the channel agents were terminated and the channel leadership and many field managers were replaced.

Lessons

Money. AT&T mismanaged a strategic market opportunity. It wasted millions and delayed the effective entry of its indirect channel program for eighteen months or more by inept executive management. Careers and businesses suffered because of this. Opportunity costs would run into the millions, as the first program derailed only to be rebuilt eventually. Additionally, AT&T tarnished its reputation in the marketplace as a predictable supplier and partner.

Politics. AT&T's direct sales organization spent time and resources to fight the indirect channel and to work for its political demise.

Along the way, the poorly managed channel conflict confused customers and diverted field management focus.

As a sales manager, you can imagine the distractions yourself. If sales reps from your larger accounts reported channel conflict in accounts assigned to your branch, you would have to rise to their defense. Alternatively, if your responsibility were in channel management, you would vigorously defend the actions of your agents, arguing that customers have the right to choose the channel from which they buy AT&T services. Channel conflict can be effective in improving account coverage, but only if well managed. An important political lesson to remember is that positioning is everything. The direct sales organization was far better positioned with decision makers at headquarters.

Selection Criteria. A key reason for the program's failure was poor qualification. For example, we determined that a site visit was essential. Its objective was to measure just four attributes that would identify agents most likely to succeed. Once a channel manager compared the prospective agent to these attributes, decisions could be made swiftly.

One "must" question was, "Is the CEO or president involved and committed to making the AT&T relationship work for both sides?" In the first go-round, the channel managers were dealing with sales and marketing people who could not make that commitment for the company. Their focus was to use the AT&T logo as a distinctive advantage in their marketing of other products. Often they would use the AT&T association as an entrée, and then sell another product in their line, which may have had a lower price or greater commission. That is why this was a "must" question. Knowing this single answer could tell us more than pages of other questions.

Under pressure and through overconfidence, managers began to introduce their own criteria. Their results were catastrophic. This argues for the thin-slicing approach for channel partner selection. A certain amount of conformity in agent profiles ensures a more consistent result. While there was simply not enough time to ramp any channel program to meet the ambitious sales objectives, channel conflict would have been minimized by more careful selection of channel partners. Another important secondary effect would have been to avoid the distraction of the political battle waged by the direct sales organization.

The 80/20 Rule

In a final take away from this experience, I want to highlight how the 80/20 rule dramatically played out with AT&T's channel. I was keynote speaker for a national training session where I displayed a fan-fold printout of all its active sales agents—about 500 of them—ranked from high to low in sales.

We drew a line on the report below the group of agents that produced 80% of the program's revenue. Then we counted from the top 100 agents (20% of 500) and drew another line. It was close to the first line. This was a textbook matchup of 20% of the people providing 80% of the result. A provocative discussion ensued on the possibilities of dropping the 80% of the agents who only deliver 20% of the results.

CHAPTER 6

Product/Market Match

Promise, large promise, is the soul of an advertisement.

SAMUEL JOHNSON

Marketing guru Ted Levitt once described the difference between marketing and sales by saying that it is sales' responsibility to get the customer to buy what the company has to sell. Today a successful sales organization defines its role well beyond this limiting description.

In industrial sales today, the smarter sales organization is the one who has a better sense of integrating sales with marketing. Customers are dealing with fewer suppliers, and businesses are adapting their company's products and services more carefully around their customers. If they can provide ideas and assistance that will help their customers become more successful, their customers will reward them.

Role of Sales

One sales leader we interviewed talked of the importance of a sales–marketing relationship. His team has responsibility approaching hundreds of millions of dollars in a single account and believes integrating marketing into the selling process is one of his keys to success. Some future-thinking students of organizational structure see sales as assuming more and more of the marketing role. It only makes sense in making every effort to win large sales and lock in customers by delivering value the customer can see. For many customers, the salesperson can add such value by incorporating marketing solutions that he or she virtually becomes the company, the brand in customers' eyes. This increasing role of the salesperson in delivering value is consistent with the need today to customize solutions such as to accommodate so-called markets of one.

This said, salespeople are not magicians. If a company does not have products that are a genuine match for customer-motivated needs, they cannot succeed. This goes to the point of the matter where earlier we noted that a particular sales group was criticized by a CFO. He said that if only salespeople would make more calls, they would make their commitment. Obviously, this is a remark made from ignorance.

A good salesman can indeed lock out competition and thereby generate revenue for some period in the decline of his or her company's products. But even the best sales organization will fail without good products.

I believe that products are the most important key to the success of any sales organization. Even with a mediocre sales organization, a company with good products can prosper. Of course, the ideal is to have great products and great distribution to become unstoppable.

Therefore, sales is at the mercy of product marketing. In many companies, there is no bridging of sales and product marketing. This is a major stake for both organizations. Repeatedly, we were told of the extraordinary loss in many organizations because sales does not provide feedback for what it sees in the marketplace. Product marketing tends to rely on data and focus groups to provide sales of products to sell. It only makes sense that each should become part of the others planning process. Why doesn't this happen?

One marketing executive told us that sales simply did not listen to marketing. He felt it was as if sales said, "just give us the product and go away. We'll figure out how to sell it."

In organizations where this mutual disrespect exists, a company could have a nation of sales reps trying to figure out for themselves which segments and target markets are best for their products. You will see this clearly in the following example. In this case, the entrepreneur has a great product, but has it targeted to the wrong market.

Unwrinkling Southern California

A plastic surgeon invested a fortune in state-of-the art laser equipment for his business. Unfortunately, he was not seeing the ROI he planned for. He had a new skin laser, which could zap wrinkles and erase skin blemishes. He saw the world as his oyster. After all, who among us doesn't have some wrinkle or other we would like to zap?

He was located in affluent southern California where the market for good looks appeared huge. He saw his target market as anyone over 40 and developed a marketing program for this mass audience. He created books of discount coupons for multiple sessions: 10 for $2,500. His advertising explained that a session was shorter than a lunch hour. His patients could go back to work without any telltale signs of their visit. He made a point of emphasizing safety. The laser was safe and FDA approved. So why were sales below expectations?

He was using marketing 101—trying to sell product features while ignoring benefits. How could he have improved his service offering?

Actually, he had a great product. However, he had not matched it with the right market. It is not enough that consumers have a *need* for your service; they must be *motivated* to address the need and have the *wherewithal* to purchase the solution.

It may be true that millions of people in Southern California over 40 have wrinkles; however, they may have no felt need to have them removed. Perhaps they hadn't even been aware that they could be removed. How could they then have been motivated to look for his product?

Another part of the product market match is having the wherewithal to buy it. Driving status automobiles is right up there with personal attractiveness for some people. Among this group, you would find folks with a high motivation to be seen in an impressive Bentley automobile. Since a Bentley may cost $150,000, motivation may mean nothing because they are missing the wherewithal to buy the car.

Professor Clayton Christensen described this need in a slightly different way: "jobs to be done"—or outcomes to achieve.[1] There is so much noise in the marketplace today that unless a person already has recognition of a need and is looking to buy a solution, there is little chance to attract his or her attention.

Christensen points out that unmotivated, unaware people are unlikely to be struck with the idea of creating a need just for your product. Over time, markets grow and more people become aware of an opportunity to address their growing needs. However, growing markets can take years to decades. This is one good reason why a sales force should have clear direction on this point. It does you no good this year or the next to have somebody addressing a market that won't be available for years. By not maintaining a good relationship with marketing, which has studied the issue and determined a target market, a sales force will squander valuable resources figuring this out for itself.

Marketing is part science and part art, and its foundation is "what customers consider value," according to Peter Drucker. "The customer never buys what the supplier sells. What is value to the customer is always something quite different from what is value or quality to the supplier."[2]

This is why focusing on the right targets in the right segment is so critical, and this is one of the key points that marketing brings to the go-to-market strategy.

Returning to our surgeon, we glimpsed what a national sales force might be like with each rep left to determine his or her own target market. It is counterintuitive to focus on a small piece of a market as you forsake the remainder of it. However, this needs to be done to succeed today where customer motivations are more finely attuned to what they need.

The surgeon could improve his focus by wrestling with the question of who, of all the people with wrinkles, would be most motivated to remove them. This would be the target market with a felt need, a job to be done, and motivation to do it.

Beauty Has Economic Value

Many studies confirm that in U.S. society physical attractiveness conveys enormous advantages to those who have it. We attribute intelligence, trust, deference, and friendliness to attractive people. Who would understand this best? It is those who once had this power, but are losing it through aging. These are the people shopping for solutions, motivated, and with the wherewithal to purchase them. Obviously, these will be the first customers in line for the surgeon's new offering. He recognized this immediately and went to work on a new marketing approach.

Now instead of advertising attributes of his service such as safety and convenience, he would appeal to the specific needs of those who were looking to hire a solution, with a job to be done. His target audience would be people who were once youthful and attractive. These people had relied on these natural advantages to earn their living or gain their station in life. These are the people who with open ears for his promise: "I restore lost beauty!"

Hindsight. In retrospect, good ideas always appear obvious. Why was this targeted approach not obvious to the surgeon? This is a common question, and I believe the answer lies in the fear of losing a larger opportunity, in this case people over 40 in Southern California. While such a market is attractive, it was never his in the first place.

Second, it is counterintuitive that revenue yield would be higher from focused marketing to fewer prospects than generalized marketing to more. This is a common mistake. For example, some sales managers claim they are vertically oriented in targeting their markets. However, they are unable to explain why they have assigned a rep to a geographical territory. The reason is that, in many cases, we are reluctant to forego the potential that may lie in this "bigger" marketplace.

Today, success seems to come from truly understanding Drucker's observation about the importance of understanding customer needs. Especially with a new product, how can one understand customer needs while chasing a broad market? Again, the response is counterintuitive. However, by focusing on fewer prospects, the company more quickly understands a market and its need for specific product attributes. Only in such a focused environment will observations rise quickly and become incorporated into a product to retain its continued competitive advantage.

Information on the target market is the job of marketing as is the requirement for good products to sell in it. As you see with the surgeon, even a product with great potential will achieve suboptimal results if targeted inappropriately. This is one more reason for both sales and marketing to become closely involved with initial planning and remain in a continuous feedback loop. It is an appropriate thing to do and for everyone's benefit.

In closing this section, let us dispel another myth that often interferes with this relationship. Business writers have said for years that customers are not the right people to ask about potential new products, since they cannot conceive of them. While this may have some generic validity, it certainly is no reason not to collaborate with marketing. I do not believe the statement represents the whole truth. Referring back to this case, customer focus groups may not have identified a laser as an attractive new product to address market needs. However, they certainly could describe attributes and features of getting rid of wrinkles, which they were looking for. Further, as customers gained more familiarity with the product, customer feedback through a selling organization can reach marketing much more quickly than it would otherwise. This is another reason for a close sales/marketing relationship. It is also another reason for today's sales organization to become more marketing oriented than yesterday's.

No Substitute for Good Products

In this situation with the surgeon, there was a market problem; however, it was one that was easily addressed. You may find that the sales organization is tasked with selling a product line at the end of its life cycle, one that is priced poorly and cannot be improved, one with the market satisfied and beginning to shrink, or a company that has no plan to launch new products to compete effectively. If your

TABLE 6.1   Market Sizing (numbers for illustration)

L.A. market	7 million people
Over 40 with wrinkles, scars, birthmarks	2.8 million (40%)
"Beautiful people" in L.A.	210,000 people (3%)
"Beautiful people" over 40	84,000 people (40%)

search turns up these situations, you have come upon Hindenburg Omens.

Sales Reach and Productivity Improve in Better-Targeted Markets

The following hypothetical example demonstrates how a shift in thinking to a better target audience produces impressive results. Your new scar and wrinkle remover business in L.A. is growing more slowly than you hoped. You have estimated there are about 7 million people in your market area and about 40% of them have a scar or wrinkles (Table 6.1). That means you have a market of 2.8 million people who need to know that you can help. Your advertising investment provides you coverage into about 30% of the

TABLE 6.2   Ineffectiveness of Random Targeting (numbers for illustration)

L.A. Market	Result
Fund sales message to achieve 30% market reach. e.g., telemarket or mail to all people over 40 years old.	840,000 people (30% of 2.8 million over 40)
However, unknown to you, only 3% are in the set of good prospects.*	25,200 people (3% of 840,000)
Best prospects identified per 100 sales contacts	3 prospects (3% effective)
Effectiveness of random targeting strategy	97% of sales effort wasted

*Well-heeled, formerly beautiful people looking to regain their good looks.

TABLE 6.3   New Strategy (numbers for illustration)

Focus effort on geographic areas with high concentration of financially able, likely appearance-conscious people, e.g., Beverly Hills	Assume new target area(s) includes 80% of desired set of prospects
Estimated good prospects reached	67,000 prospects in ZIP 90210
Best prospects identified per 100 sales contacts	40 prospects
Effectiveness of new strategy	13 times more prospects identified per 100 calls

market (Table 6.2). It dawns on you that only a small percentage of those 2.8 million people are looking for wrinkle relief, and many cannot afford your service. You conclude that your best prospects are well-heeled, formerly beautiful people looking to regain their good looks. You review the numbers to discover a much smaller universe than you earlier believed: just 84,000 people, but still more than enough to succeed (Table 6.3).

It is obvious that careful targeting produces dramatically better results. Often we do not provide our salespeople with the insights to help them improve their targeting. Industry specialization is one approach to do this.

CHAPTER 7

Competition

Never meet anybody after two for lunch. Meet in the morning because you are sharper. Never have long lunches. They're not only boring, but dangerous because of the martinis.

JOSEPH P. KENNEDY

Learning from the Fosbury Flop

We are familiar with famous names like Digital Equipment, Howard Johnson, General Motors, and others that lost their edge or became obsolete by failing to react to competitive activity. Competitors bring change, and change can be lethal to our companies. Yet, Peter Drucker observes that competition is one of the things we know least about.

Historically, business in any industry might be described as punctuated equilibrium. Things go along steady state for a while, then there is a disruptive technology that portends big trouble for those not on the "S" curve of change early enough.

Competition is one of those areas driving Ray Kurzweil's observation that change is changing at an exponential rate.[1] The Internet has democratized information today. Nearly anyone can find information about any subject online. To prove the point, the U.S. government inadvertently posted captured Iraqi plans for an atom bomb on the net, available to any surfer until they were suddenly removed.

Invisible Competitors

A former professor at Harvard observed that there is always some new kid in his dorm room practicing to be the fastest gun in the west. We know that is the story of how Michael Dell began to take over an industry as an undergraduate. With information available and competitors often invisible, the business world is less predictable. Indeed, can we even define what constitutes an industry— even when we are in it?

In all of this, there are some predictable patterns in how a disruptive competitive technology emerges, gains a foothold, and eventually displaces the old technology. I will use an Olympic athletic event to show how this happens.

The high jump became an Olympic event in the late 1800s, about the same time Bell invented the telephone. Since then the high jump evolved through several cycles of change in which competitors developed new technology to challenge the old ways and then obsolete them.

The first Olympic high jumpers employed a technique called the scissors. They ran to the bar and leaped, putting one leg forward over the bar, then the other. The scissors became the technique (technology) used by everyone for decades until the Western Roll became popular in the 1930s. To execute the Western Roll, jumpers threw their bodies into a roll parallel to the bar.

When the roll emerged as a new jumping technology, the best jumpers were still scissors jumpers, and they pooh-poohed the roll. Others saw potential in the roll and worked diligently to learn it. Scissors jumpers redoubled their effort, but improvement was slow. The roll technique had more upside potential, and in time achieved heights no scissors jumper could match.

Years later, the Straddle jump gained popularity. The Straddle jumper leapt over the bar with his chest down, pulling his stomach over the bar. The Straddle appeared to provide incremental improvement for those who invested in learning it. Others decided to stay with the Western Roll after observing that the competitive advantage of the Straddle was unclear. There was simply not enough evidence to give up the old way.

Western Rollers were convinced that their new technique would supplant the old. Just as before, those who held to the old technology reached the limit of their technology and became obsolete. The Straddle demonstrated continuous improvement and reached heights impossible for rollers to achieve.

In the 1960s a new technique again displaced the old. It was a strange, eponymic technique dubbed the Fosbury Flop. An unknown kid named Dick Fosbury emerged from his proverbial dorm room in the Pacific Northwest with a new jumping technology to challenge the jumping world.

Fosbury struggled learning the Straddle technique. One day he decided to run at the bar, jump and twist his body to go over the bar backwards with his chest facing up. He sort of flopped over the bar.

You can guess what the Straddlers and jumping fans did when they first saw the Fosbury Flop. They howled at his inelegant and improbable technique. Of course, we know how the story ends. Fosbury won the gold medal in the Olympic high jump in Mexico in 1968. Today everybody flops.

Lessons

There are some interesting lessons here for sales forces as well as companies. First, competitive change appears only incremental when first introduced. Additionally, the competition may appear far less sophisticated than the existing competitive services.

"Incremental" and "less sophisticated" are probably valid descriptions of early competitive changes. The serious mistake to beware is underestimating the future of a disruptive change. A disruptive change is a punctuation point in the competitive equilibrium where new technology changes the market direction.

The early telephone and subsequent growth of AT&T parallel the cycles of entry and decay we discussed in Olympic competition. Technology makes a modest entry, gains acceptance by enthusiastic outsiders who see potential, then morphs and develops in unexpected ways, dethroning the old guard as it does.

Competitors who observe the unsophisticated state of a new market introduction often believe that by working harder at their own technique or technology, they can overcome the challenge. Ignoring promising competition by digging your own heels in to make incremental improvements in your own technology can be a fatal mistakes.

Training yourself to be a close observer of change is one way to keep your career in shape. One easy way to do this is called horizon scanning.

All that's required is:

- Selecting a topic(s) to focus on.
- Setting up a file folder and/or a computer file for each topic.
- Searching for and clipping new information at least monthly, or clipping whenever you happen across information serendipitously.

Try these free/inexpensive tools help:

- EverNote, a note organizer and clipper (evernote.com), is a nifty way to clip, store, organize, and recall your information.
- Yahoo permits you to store key search words for your topics.
- StumbleUpon.com will surprise you with unknown, helpful websites on your topic.
- And, of course, there's Google and a raft of add-ins for search specialties.

This is the same approach many futurists use to keep their eye on ideas and trends just over the horizon. It's a tool that will enhance your own career as you develop a reputation for identifying "predictable surprises" early enough for your company to act on the intelligence. Finally, scanning the horizon is a smart way to maintain a personal focus upon changing markets and technology that will structure your future. Alternatively, you can await the future passively. In sales management, passivity is almost never a good strategy.

History Repeats Competitive Ebbs and Flows

*Can anyone remember when times weren't hard
and money not scarce?*

RALPH WALDO EMERSON

Our story begins at an early 1800s inflection point, the Industrial Revolution. Just after our Revolutionary War, and still smarting from defeat, the British retained their commercial supremacy through knowledge of waterpower and manufacturing. Britain ruled the world in manufacturing and production of textiles and was determined to keep its intellectual property secrets to itself. The Brits guarded their written plans and would not allow even sketches of the workings of their water-powered textile mills. Workers familiar with this technology were prohibited from leaving the country. After all, the last thing Britain wanted was competition from us upstarts in the United States. Britain's worry was well founded, for subsequent events in the United States established what happens when industrious opportunists get hold of your secrets.

Technology Disintermediates Industries

Slater's Mill, built in 1793, was the spark that ignited the Industrial Revolution in the United States. Samuel Slater was a mid-level manager in Britain's Arkwright textile mills. Even with all precautions, Britain could not guard its intellectual secrets from the magnificent memory of Slater, who covertly immigrated to America. He found financial backers, and with sketches redrawn from memory as both machine and mill construction manager, he created the mill that launched the U.S. industrial revolution.

Slater's textile mill had just thirteen employees, but could not keep its operations secret either. By the 1870s, at the end of the Industrial Revolution, there were more than 850 textile mills in New

England. With textiles available in the United States, it was no longer necessary to rely on imported goods.

Other changes in U.S. business were just as profound. The railroad took flour ground by steel rollers in large mills like Pillsbury's to small towns throughout the United States. Every local miller was suddenly in an occupation with precipitously declining sales and no way to match the prices of large producers. Itinerant millstone grinders were in a dying occupation as were so many others as the Industrial Revolution changed the United States permanently.

Today's information revolution is another inflection point with changes unimaginable to the last generation of sales representatives. The Industrial Revolution was about producing and selling huge quantities of tangible goods produced at unimaginably low prices. The information revolution is about selling the intangible.

Global Competition 1840s' Style

Technological competition is not the only change driver. Global competition is nothing new either. In the 1840s, Henry David Thoreau in Concord, Massachusetts, was doing more than living alone in his hut on Walden Pond. In a little-known business cameo, including R&D, operations, and sales prowess, he saved his family pencil-making business from foreign competition.

The British began selling better-made pencils than those made in the United States, including the Thoreau family's. In an exemplary display of a can-do attitude, Thoreau walked the 24-mile round trip to the Harvard Library several times to research the competition. There, he dug out ideas from German chemistry papers, another example of effective use of someone else's intellectual property. He tweaked his supply chain by shifting to a new graphite supplier, and voila! Thoreau created a new product line with soft and hard leads. He also invented a drill that allowed his family company to slide lead into the shaft rather than opening and regluing the entire pencil shaft. Then, he and his dad went on a sales trip to New York City to relaunch their product line by selling door-to-door in Manhattan. The company was saved, and Thoreau left the business. It was not long, however, before imports rose again as serious competitors.

Of course, globalization has morphed since Thoreau's time. Today, global commerce includes information, capital, manufacturing, and even services. Fred Smith, CEO of FedEx, says the trend in global trade is toward high-value products like semiconductor chips, designer clothing, and auto parts. Former Fed Chairman Alan Greenspan observes that the aggregate output of the United States is five times greater in real terms than in 1950. Fred Smith adds that that output weighs exactly the same—not a pound more in the last fifty years.[2]

Manufacturing employment is only about 10% of the U.S. work-force today. Little remains to outsource. Now, the heat is on white-collar workers. As far as most people believed, services were white-collar tasks that could not trade across borders. The Internet and communications advances stomped on the maxim that services were strictly local.

Technology now enables us to sell by email at $.10 per contact and by telemarketing $1.00 per contact. The cost of a face-to-face sales call is minimally estimated at $250, far higher than in Thoreau's time. At today's costs, much of what used to be sales force work such as customer care is performed more economically with technology in call centers around the world. With perhaps 7 million pages a day of new product on the Internet, sales will change in ways unseen today. Communications is cheap, and any worker in the world can be virtually anywhere. E-based delivery and sales capabilities can deliver many services wherever they are required.

Conventional wisdom and guidelines continue to melt. Historically, the rule has been that only small companies should use agents to market their products. Companies that had technical products sold direct. Today sales agents can go to market as effectively as direct sales organizations, often with greater scope, flexibility, and coverage.[3]

And so, the shape of traditional sales forces continues to change. To see where change takes us, we must be on our tiptoes, scanning the horizon, alert and ready to change our businesses and ourselves. Just as business strategies change, so must our personal strategies. A superb personal strategy for the past may be worthless the day after tomorrow. All of us in sales know that we can't stand still. Who hasn't been reminded, "those were last month's results. The important question is what are you going to sell this month?"

Personal Upgrades

Senior sales executives whose once most valuable stock in trade—intuition and judgment—may be criticized as relics of the past. Your problem may be one of perception, not competence. You may have the right answers, but be unable to explain your decisions using the latest business school jargon. Hence, to colleagues from a different generation it may appear that your skills are outdated.

For new sales managers, the up-and-comers, your decisions tend to be prompt and decisive. Your energy and enthusiasm can land you in trouble for jumping too quickly to shortsighted decisions. Your task is to accumulate experience and intuition as quickly as possible.

Many mid-level sales executives anxiously hope to maintain career momentum. They will push ahead or be stuck where they are for the remainder of their careers.

More Help Required

Sales needs more help and more friends. Many highly touted solutions du jour have not met expectations. With all the emphasis and money spent on CRM, quality, customer-focused marketing, and consultative selling, it is startling to see surveys reporting the following:

- Just 20% of your customers are happy with their sales rep assigned to them.[4]
- Senior management sees sales management as underperforming.[5]
- Sales management has shortest employment tenure of all corporate departments.[6]
- Selling ranks at the bottom of consumer perception of honesty and ethical standards.[7]
- 49% of managers knew reps lied to make a sale.[8]

- And in one of the unkindest cuts of all, your own reps are unhappy with their sales management.[9]

Field Skills Needed

Solutions will not come from headquarters. AT&T used to issue 32 linear feet of binders to branch offices with "general instructions." I never found answers in them. Even newly updated, they contained relatively few answers for the field. The field has different problems.

Your big challenges are situational. You must be a real-time field leader who engages competition as you meet it and marshals the capabilities of your company to support the sales force here and now.

To do this, a sales manager needs the perspective of an economist, the facility with detail of a corporate controller, the skill of an industrial psychologist to motivate reps, the insights of Dale Carnegie for colleagues and superiors, and the Wisdom of Solomon.

With all these exigencies, performance pressure, and conflicting goals, sales management is an especially tough place to be today. That is why I wrote this book.

CHAPTER 8

The Customer

He that wrestles with us strengthens our nerves, and sharpens our skill. Our antagonist is our helper.

EDMUND BURKE, 1790

Customers have changed. After all, they face the same challenges we all do: squeezed margins, increased competition, and everything else related to faster changing change. They are more heterogeneous than ever, and the trend is ever more so toward "markets of one." Relationships still matter, but in a different way. Rather than Willie Loman's "personal" relationships being paramount, it's "business" relationships that take precedence today.

There are still differences from one continent to another. U.S. sales executives told us that there is much more emphasis on proving the financial return of any investment. In Europe the trend in buying decisions is headed toward more objectivity and less customer loyalty. Nevertheless, a good relationship still trumps incremental improvements in products or ROIs. It takes more than a slight competitive edge for a company to abandon a good vendor relationship.

In an example of the decline of vendor loyalty in the United States, some companies use technology to help them better rationalize their supply chains. We talked to salespeople at SAS Institute who told us that customers buy their software to consolidate supply chains. One client found over 5,000 vendors providing products and services to its locations throughout North America. Using software, the client can combine same vendor purchases to gain discounts and other advantages with the seller. For instance, a mega-buyer can demand that a supplier develop new marketing programs every thirty days to keep its products fresh—and moving.

In industrial sales, power still flows to the buyer. A sales VP at a major international technology firm described the downstream effect at his company of customers consolidating their supply lines. "There are fewer customers, but bigger customers," he said. "Sometimes this means windfall revenue when a client takes money from a smaller supplier and applies it to products and services of a preferred vendor.

"However, this is a two-edged sword, for with the additional revenue comes additional responsibility."

Loyalty Costs More Now

Some accounts become just too large to lose no matter what resources must be pumped in protect them. Solid business relationships are costly. With large bulwarks of resources protecting key accounts, competitors find it difficult and expensive to make inroads. However, customers have practiced strategies to keep incumbents on their toes.

Customers want to be certain they are always buying value and continue to test their strategic vendors to assure themselves that that remains so. One tactic to keep a preferred vendor on its toes is to continually test for value by creating RFPs for large pieces of add-on business. We found even well-positioned vendors complaining about their customers' reliance on RFPs as a measure of due diligence. While this practice may have the desired effect of consistently assessing value, there are some drawbacks.

The practice adds additional costs to the system. The incumbent vendor and customer must apply resources to the effort of producing and managing the response process for the new RFP. The customer must also entice outside vendors to bid on the project. This increases those vendors' costs also. Sometimes, an outside vendor must be cajoled into bidding because of the likelihood that it has no genuine opportunity to win the bid, as discussed in other chapters of this book. Be certain to read the next section closely for counter-tactics when you suspect that you may be a predesignated loser.

Customers are the ultimate judges of your go-to-market program. Stay close to them. Ask them frankly about your service to them. How do they compare you to your competition? Do they see the same trends you see as you scan the horizon for change? After you have done this, evaluate as adequate or inadequate your company's relationship with its customers.

How to Avoid Being the Designated Loser

> *I don't know the key to success, but the key to failure is trying to please everybody.*
>
> BILL COSBY

The last time his contract came up for renewal, there was a big hul-labaloo about whether David Letterman would leave CBS for ABC. Millions of dollars were at stake for both networks. By becoming the center of a bidding war, Letterman gained leverage to play the bid-ders against each other, and then pocketed millions staying put at CBS. A critic observed that if CBS had simply put the pieces together, it would have realized ABC's scheduling couldn't possibly please Letterman. He speculated that ABC was being shopped by Letterman to pressure CBS. We will never know the whole story, but we do know Letterman's tactic succeeded.

In today's marketplace, prospects use the same tactic against service provider account executives, and it works well there, too. My research shows at least half the proposals created are submitted for deals where a competitor was predetermined to win. The prospect was simply shopping around to compare its preferred vendor's price to "keep them honest" or to gain leverage to drive it down.

Proposal Win Rate

I studied 707 proposals generated over four consecutive quarters by a company that sold network and call center services and telecom/IT infrastructure support. The sales vice president was proud that his organization was winning twice as many deals as it lost, doubling the past year's win rate. Unfortunately, he was still way behind his revenue quota.

The study produced the following initial results: 212 wins (30 percent), 106 losses (15 percent) and 389 no decision/pending (55 percent). "Wins" and "losses" speak for themselves, but what is a "no decision"? When the reps updated the true status of these pending proposals, we found only 6 would be won, and 383 actually would be lost. The conclusion was obvious to the sales vice president: "We were being shopped more than half the time."

In other words, the average account executive spent 110 days—50 percent of his or her time—to provide pricing for prospects that never intended to buy. When we added in the thousands of support days burned, travel expenses, and opportunity costs, the total cost became staggering.

How large is this waste of resources in your sales organization? How great are the possibilities for sales growth if even a portion of this resource drain were applied to real selling opportunities?

This chapter addresses three areas to improve targeting sales opportunities:

1. Guiding principles to identify situations where you are being shopped.
2. Weighing evidence to determine if it is a fair opportunity to win.
3. Improving the odds of winning in a questionable situation.

Guiding Principles

Shoppers easily disguise their true intent, since account executives, pressured to keep the sales funnel full, do not often ask tough questions to qualify opportunities. Shoppers have ready answers for:

Who will be making the final decision? . . . "Me"

Is the money budgeted? . . . "Yes"

When will the decision be made? . . . "Soon"

Does anyone have the inside track? . . . "No"

The principle to apply here is that actions speak louder than words. A prospect that needs your price "by Friday" and claims you do not need to talk to anyone else is behaving in a way that belies his or her words that "everyone has a fair chance." In addition, your antennae should go up if an unsolicited request comes from someone who is not already a customer. You should calculate the odds of winning a large piece of business from someone with whom you have no relationship. Instead, you start to dream about how enormous the opportunity is and how you're going to spend your bonus check. Why would you want to press too hard with qualifying questions that might upset the prospect?

As a rule, you are well positioned in a deal if you are in a consultative mode and helping to shape the buying process. Here are some customer behaviors you may observe to confirm your feeling at the outset:

- The prospect probably was not "looking" before you called.
- You spark interest and shape the opportunity.
- Timeframes are reasonable.
- There is open discussion.
- The prospect is open to any good ideas.
- Your contact introduces you to the decision maker.

In the closing phase of the deal:

- The buyer still is open to your influence.
- The buyer remains inquisitive.
- The decision maker is involved.
- The prospect brings up non-service/product issues that broaden involvement.
- The prospect promises you the last shot.
- You have access to the key people.

Therefore, even without asking where you stand, the prospect's behavior gives you clues about your competitive position. Unfortunately, many of us are not good observers and are pulled easily into a shopping situation.

In *Mozart's Brain and the Fighter Pilot* by Richard Restak[1] we learn our brains are made to resolve ambiguity quickly, leading us to jump to conclusions that fit the evidence we see. For example, you observe that all your phone calls are returned promptly, and all your questions about the deal are answered quickly. You could decide that you are being treated as if you have an edge.

However, these same observations also support the hypothesis that you are being shopped. Your calls may be answered quickly in order not to slow the process, not because the buyer is motivated to find the best solution. To get a better sense of where you stand, look for behaviors inconsistent with a level playing field. Why? They can kill a hypothesis rather than support it.

For example, if you are being shopped, you would have a sense the buying process controls you:

- You had no influence in developing the need.
- Prospect requires an unusually quick response ("Just to get a ballpark price, then we can talk").
- The scope of specs is limiting.
- You cannot talk to the decision maker ("She will just rubber-stamp my decision anyway").
- All they ask are product/service questions. They could be shopping for a stove rather than a business partner relationship.
- You are told, "You have a good shot," when you are not sure you even understand their business.
- Your inquiries are answered quickly to keep the process moving.
- They say, "Give us your best and final offer," which is hardly a collaborative stance.

Weigh the Evidence

A hypothesis is a statement that has not been established as true. People determine if they believe a hypothesis by the weight of supporting evidence, but a hypothesis cannot be conclusively proven true. For centuries people believed the Earth was flat, and they had plenty of evidence to support their belief. When Magellan sailed around the world, the flat-world hypothesis was shown to be false. You can apply this approach to assessing an RFP in the same manner that Magellan's feat proved the Earth was round. You need only a single strong piece of contradictory evidence to show a hypothesis is false.

With an RFP, there are two hypotheses:

1. You have a fair chance to compete.
2. You do not have a fair chance to compete.

To test these hypotheses against a current situation, draw a matrix like the one in Table 8.1 and label the columns as shown. List significant factors you think have a major effect on the outcome of the bid down the left-hand column. Focus on behavior observed

TABLE 8.1 Testing a Hypothesis

Evidence	We have a fair chance to win	We are being shopped
Two week deadline for proposal	I	C
CEO is former colleague of competitor	I	C
Initial RFP was a surprise	I	C
Limited scope of the proposal— unwilling to broaden scope	I	C
$100M decision: "They will rubberstamp my decision"	I	C
Questions answered promptly; no time lost	C	C
Transactional/Product-type questions	I	C
Surprise—at the presentation, they changed the criteria	I	C
Prospect keeps affirming, "You have a good shot"	C	C

rather than talk. Now, work across for each factor and note if it is "C" consistent or "I" inconsistent with the hypothesis above. What do you conclude when you work through the evidence? The hypothesis with the *least compelling inconsistent* evidence should become your preferred hypothesis.

While all the factors are consistent with "We are being shopped," this is not conclusive, because consistent information often supports several hypotheses. The inconsistent information is much more telling. The weight of this evidence screams the hypothesis "We have a fair chance to compete" is unlikely. Therefore, the favored hypothesis is "We are being shopped."

Advice for Your Salespeople about RFPs

First, become familiar with the thin-slicing technique in Chapter 4.

If you get an unexpected RFP, assume you are being shopped. Determine where you stand by weighing evidence using the test described above. Show your manager your conclusion and get his or her agreement to support you if you decide not to bid or to use a strategy such as the following.

Tell the prospect it is your company policy not to create a proposal without at least three interviews with executives affected by the decision. If you will expend effort, they must demonstrate their sincerity, too. It is absurd to think you can develop an excellent proposal for someone's unique business requirements without doing this.

If you are denied the interviews, write them declining their request to bid. Use this as an opportunity to communicate your sincere intentions around their business. Copy several executives and briefly describe your results at similar companies.

If you get the interviews you request, ask questions to assess what needs executives have beyond those outlined in the RFP. Ask what would solve their problems. If you have solutions, you can take a giant step toward leveling the playing field by enrolling that executive as a supporter of the new capability you can provide that is not called for in the RFP. You want to create your own edge over the incumbent or intended recipient of the business.

Answer the RFP, adding in your cover letter and executive summary that your proposal provides a superior solution, since it addresses critical needs and solutions beyond those identified in the RFP. Outline how you plan to address these needs with your services. Estimate the ROI of your new solution to demonstrate it is a compelling offer. Develop your solution in the proposal. Copy the executive whose needs you have addressed and follow up with others who seemed supportive.

Now, compete on the new field you created!

CHAPTER 9

The Market

There is one thing stronger than all the armies in the world, and that is an idea whose time has come.

VICTOR HUGO

In time, every product reaches the end of its life cycle and no longer maintains its product/market match. Sales is usually the first to discover this and bring back the bad news from the marketplace. Changes like this do not happen overnight, but build like avalanches from changes in competition, regulation, the economy or customer needs.

Sales Is Only the Messenger

The sales department cannot change markets. It must take markets as it finds them, succeeding by adapting its tactics to the environment. If a company's product and tactics happen to be an effective match for the market, times will be good. You have probably witnessed success in some markets where a company had a good product but a marginal sales organization and still succeeded. Timing and random chance can turn average people into stars. The reverse is also true. Competent managers fail because of bad luck or being at the wrong company at the wrong time. There is also the explanation offered that success breeds failure. That is because we are unable to see changes that are incompatible with our past success patterns. A remarkable example of this occurred with the Digital Equipment Corporation (DEC).

DEC's mini computers enjoyed phenomenal growth in the beginning in the 1960s and peaking in 1990. Its PDP and VAX computers opened computing to millions of companies that were too small for IBM's mainframes. DEC competed on overall cost and technology. Its sales force enjoyed a powerful product/market match so good that DEC paid its salespeople flat salaries. Then PC technology changed the market. DEC's proprietary software and commitment to a proprietary Alpha chip skewed its product/market match. It had fine products, but its market declined. By the time this was clear, DEC missed the PC market altogether.

Regrettably, its CEO said he could not foresee the need people could have for PCs in their homes and offices. However competent DEC's sales force, it had no power to change the market's direction. The sales force was just the canary in the mine reporting a Hindenburg Omen back to the CEO who would not see it.

DEC's old headquarters is just a few miles from me. Ken Olson, DEC's founder and longtime CEO, began the company's rise from a modest corner office on the ground floor of an old Civil War blanket mill directly on the main street. Olson remained there even when his original team of 117 people in 1957 grew to more than 120,000 in 1990. This humility and accessibility contributed to the unusual engineering culture. DEC was one of the early companies where employees could dress casually every day. People loved to work for him.

When things began to change, I imagine there were some bone-crunching discussions in that office on Main Street. Perhaps DEC's VP of Sales was instructed, "You sales guys committed to the number. Make more calls and get more into the funnel." Would more pressure on the sales force have helped? What if they added commissions to the compensation plan? Is there anything DEC might have done to convince millions of businesses that PCs were a passing fad? A CSO can alter the field's tactics only for a brief time and only so far to forestall the inevitable product/market dissolution.

DEC's failure was not unique. Markets have shifted for thousands of years. When bad news comes as a surprise and when there are no new products and services ready for a counterassault, no one wants to hear that the company's market is in decline. Denial is the common reaction when sales delivers this message. It is unpleasant news for any CEO. Several CEOs told us why they do not trust sales to make market assessments. In the first place, sales is not an impartial observer. If sales claims the market is declining, these CEOs suspect the observation to be a self-serving excuse to back away from a revenue commitment.

CEOs also say sales tends to use anecdotal evidence rather than well-researched business cases to present its claim. Third, the sales department does not coordinate its resources to present a unified position. Sales tends to complain one person at a time. CEOs hear concerns in dribs and drabs at the water cooler, in field visits, or in meetings. Often sales misses the big picture entirely because it does not present a well-researched, quantified case.

The CEO may ask a rep why sales are down and get an opinion that sales would improve if only this attribute or that attribute were added to the product. Hint to CEOs: When reps talk about adding attributes, the product may be too long in the tooth to save.

CEOs want a comprehensive business case and alternatives for something as serious as a market change. They prefer the hard research that the marketing department provides them. Of course, marketing's information may not be any more accurate than sales' anecdotes. However, perception is important. CEOs like numbers, and value is in the eye of the beholder.

In the next example of a market change, senior management provided the field organization with the power of inquisition, torture, and even death to achieve revenue results. We will see if even these tactics can save a market once it is gone.

The Great Market Shift in 100 CE

For thousands of years, managers have struggled to convince their superiors that markets change, and therefore expectations of markets must change as well. It has never been easy to convince the boss to settle for less revenue this year when he got more last year. I want to share the one classic case where this happened.

I was in church listening to a sermon, when I first learned about one of history's most successful bids for a revenue quota reduction. Pliny, who received the quota reduction, had two strong forces in his favor. First, Pliny was no slacker when pursuing his objectives, and second, there was no disputing that the market had changed forever.

Trajan and Pliny the Younger

Trajan was a popular emperor of the Roman Empire at the turn of the second century. In 111 CE, he named Pliny the Younger governor of Pontus and Bithynia (modern Turkey). We know much about Pliny because he compiled volumes of his letters and writings.

Pliny's Problem

Puzzling changes were occurring in Pliny's territory. Tax revenues fell, and attendance declined at pagan temples. In turn, poor attendance caused declining revenue from the purchase of meat from temple sacrifices.

There were more problems. Worst of these was a steady drop in tax receipts from the tinsmiths. They produced likenesses of Pliny's boss the Emperor and other idols for worship.

No one wants to report a revenue shortfall, especially when your boss is the Emperor of the Roman Empire. I can imagine what was going on in Pliny's mind. I'm sure he felt worse because of the decline in worship of the emperor himself. He must have felt stress as he wondered how to explain these results.

Hundreds of thousands of sales executives have been in parallel situations. They had the choice of two roads they might take. One road denies reality and is traveled by those with unwarranted optimism. Too many managers take this road because their judgment is poor or because they believe sales executives ought to have "can do" attitudes in the face of any odds. Managers who see reality take the other road.

Pliny might have taken the first road. He could have assured the Emperor that things would be back on track by the next quarter.

That is always a tempting short-term stress reliever. However, Pliny suspected that the changes in Pontus and Bithynia were permanent.

He knew that another inaccurate forecast would kill his credibility. More bad numbers might earn him the dubious distinction of an invitation to Rome for a personal presentation to the Emperor. The long horse ride to Rome would rekindle the stress and a strong suspicion that he was a short-timer.

Perhaps he would get another chance. More likely, the Emperor would explain to Pliny how his shortfall jeopardized important projects and plans. Then Trajan would have put his arm around Pliny's shoulders, walked him over to the window, and pulled the curtain for Pliny to observe the lions in the Coliseum below. That would tacitly underscore Pliny's requirement to "manage to commitment."

Pliny was a bright man who knew the certain consequences of creating false expectations. No, Pliny must have thought, it was a fool's plan to promise that the numbers would improve in the next quarter. He chose the second road: to know the truth and tell the truth, letting the chips fall where they may. Today we call his approach managing-up.

First, he gathered good intelligence on his Christian competition by torturing several deaconesses. He learned that their religion prohibited them from worshiping idols and attending pagan temples. Christians avoided the markets where sacrificed meat was sold.

Next, he launched militant countermeasures to turn his subjects around. Despite all his effort in communicating displeasure at Christian practices, he conceded that his plan improved temple attendance by only a small number. More dramatic measures did not improve results.

Finally, he wrote to Trajan explaining his aggressive actions and admitting marginal results to restore tax receipts and return worship of the emperor to its previous level. Pliny did not perceive the scope of his problem at the time. He happened to be governor of the fastest growing Christian community of the age.

"I interrogated these as to whether they were Christians; those who confessed I interrogated a second and a third time, threatening them with punishment; those who persisted I ordered executed."

The Emperor connected with this vivid picture of Pliny's commitment to achieving his objectives. Then, he added an embellishment. Pliny respectfully stated, "It is my practice, my lord, to refer to you all matters concerning which I am in doubt. For who can better give guidance to my hesitation or inform my ignorance?" Even then, flattery was effective in managing-up.

Trajan replied giving Pliny an "attaboy." "You observed proper procedure, my dear Pliny. . . ." The Emperor agreed that the world had changed, at least on Pliny's side of the Black Sea. He advised Pliny to back off his plan to kill the remaining Christians. "For this is both a dangerous kind of precedent and out of keeping with the spirit of our age." The wise Trajan saw that resistance to the changes was futile.

This predicament of the Emperor and Governor Pliny holds a critical caveat for sales executives valid today. Once an organization stumbles and growth is stalled, you must be extremely careful in accepting the challenge to come aboard to turn sales around. According to a study, *Stall Points,* published by the Corporate Strategy Board in 1998, "probably the most daunting challenge in delivering growth is that if you fail once to deliver it, the odds that you ever will be able to deliver in the future are very low."[1] The study examined 172 compaines from *Fortune's* list of the 50 largest companies between 1955 and 1995. Ninety-five percent of these companies seemed to run out of oxygen and to stall at or below the rate of growth of our GNP (gross national product). It is far more likely that market and not leadership was the cause of failure to reignite growth in these companies. It is a low probability coincidence that 95% of these companies had incompetent sales and other senior executives. Just as in our case above, circumstances almost always trump individuals.

What is the market situation for your company? Is it growing or shrinking? Rate the market as adequate or inadequate to succeed.

Personal Coaching

PART II

Personal Coaching

CHAPTER 10

Facts-in-the-Future™

It is not certain that everything is uncertain.

PASCAL, *PENSEES*, 1670

Consider the Odds, Charlie Brown

I have seen a recurring *Peanuts* episode of Lucy holding a football and encouraging Charlie Brown to kick it. Charlie always gets suckered in, for just as he runs to kick the ball, Lucy always moves it. A surprised Charlie always kicks only air and lands on his bottom. Because we are familiar with Lucy's ploy, we grin as she suckers Charlie in—again each fall as the cartoon is reprised.

Predictable Surprises

If you were Charlie, and had seen this pattern before, you would know that only two things could happen. Either Lucy will hold the ball and let him kick it, or she will move it at the last minute. Lucy always moves it. Therefore, the next time you saw the cartoon, you would be highly certain that her behavior would repeat itself. There are some facts in the future.

If Charlie thought beyond his immediate desire to give the ball a good kick, he might have considered the odds that Lucy would let him do it. Lucy had two choices. She could hold the ball for Charlie to kick, or move it at the last second and watch the fun. Charlie's reflexive inclination is to give the ball a good kick. Will he ever learn?

Like Charlie Brown, most of us could benefit from using simple tools like mindfulness, horizon scanning, applying simple statistics and probability (Chapter 11), and more, as you will see ahead, to become better predictors of our future by making better decisions today. As I said in the Introduction, you do not control all the levers for your own success; however, because you control your own mindset and outlook, you surely can change your future. You can improve your odds of creating a future you want. I wrote this book to add practical tools and insights to succeed even when someone like Lucy is holding the ball.

I know there are some skeptics who may believe that the future is preordained. I think that this chapter is a critical decision point for them. They can remain powerless at the mercy of the circumstances or change their path of least resistance by striking out on their own course for a better future. This is the biggest no-brainer in the history of sales management. Let me explain why, beginning with some general discussion about predicting the future and then moving on specifically to sales management.

Predicting the future may raise the specter of crystal balls and clairvoyance. After all, no one ever knows what will really happen in the future. Nevertheless, you already take your best shot at doing it every day as a function of your experience, and you are not alone:

- All science is based upon prediction . . . if A, then B.
- U.S. business spends hundreds of millions on analysts who use time-tested tools to predict things like the size of markets.
- Hundreds of millions of dollars is paid to economists whose guesses about the future are the basis of corporate and government plans.
- Baseball batters study pitchers for tip-offs about their next pitch. They are not right every time, but even a slight edge in their

predictive power pays enormous benefits for their batting averages and pay envelopes.

- We rely on meterologists' forecasts for many of our plans. They are often wrong, but we play the odds.
- Governments adjust security levels as a function of their prediction of terrorist activity.
- Even animals predict the future, as they store food preparing for the certain winter.

The notion of predicting something is not such a radical idea, as we see in the examples above. The dictionary simply defines prediction as a foretelling based on observation, experience, or reasoning. The most successful sales managers know that thinking about the future is essential to every aspect of their job. Hockey great Wayne Gretzky explained the difference between average and successful in his industry: "A good hockey player plays where the puck is. A great hockey player plays where the puck is going to be." Anticipation, said guru Peter Drucker, is the number one skill for managing well in turbulent times.

Change Accelerates

In my research, I traveled to hear futurist and best-selling author Ray Kurzweil speak about the future and his newest book *The Singularity Is Near*.[1] He has observed that the world is not just changing; it is changing at an exponential rate. In other words, change is speeding up. In the 1900s we saw the previous equivalent of 100 years change every 24 years. Therefore, while change is nothing new, Kurzweil's insight is that we have far less time than before to anticipate and adapt to change before new change arrives. He promises we will have even less time in the future.

Of course, all change involves risk. Our key concern is minimizing risk by making better decisions. This is one of the main themes in *The Sales Manager's Success Manual*. There is no avoiding risk, and since it will always be present we believe that the best strategy is to address the future with eyes open to risks and rewards.

As a side note, in *Against the Gods,*[2] Peter Bernstein argues that the dividing line beginning modern society is the understanding of risk. Pre-modern man relied upon subjective guess about the risk of a future activity. Today with modern methods of analysis we can predict the future pretty well in some areas.

We know how long people will live, on average (now 78 in the United States). We understand the odds of having a boy or girl or of the Red Sox winning the World Series. As with the Red Sox, sometimes even simple statistics help us make a safe bet up to 99% of the time!

Anticipating the Future

Author Jack Wilner wrote: "Sales managers who have vision can predict the future—simply because they create it!"[3] Let me add that there are many CEOs who demand that their sales managers have a perfect vision of the future. Why else would they demand that sales forecasts be chiseled into stone?

There are many more reasons why sales managers ought to spend more time thinking about the future:

- Thinking about the past is not productive, and the present is so fleeting that it's only logical to consider what we can do about what is going to happen.

- Sales managers who carry negative attitudes about the future consider themselves helpless to alter it, according to psychologist Martin Seligman. Perceiving yourself as a victim of the future is a self-fulfilling prophecy.

- Albert Bandura, another psychologist, adds to this observation. High self-efficacy sales managers are those who believe that they have a high level of control over the future. If they set a goal to close a major recount, they don't do it unless they believe they can. By contrast, those who see themselves as victims tend to be those who are fatalistic about the future. When something bad appears to be happening, they tend to halt their pursuit, withdraw, or quit because of their pessimism.

- Another psychologist, Noelle Nelson, believes that a person characterized as a winner is one who believes he or she has the power to reach goals. Sales managers who feel in control of their destiny have better mental health and less depression than those who succumb to pessimism and apathy.

Professor Tom Lombardo wrote in the World Future Society's *Futurist*[4] about how we can keep ourselves positive and with a sense of control. He said, "expanded foresight, goal setting, planning, and goal directed behavior give a person a sense of increased empowerment." This is an important observation, since it provides a set of actions that one can take to strengthen performance or help doubts ease. Engage in activity, he suggests, that has predictable results. In other words, winners and pessimists gain traction by taking positive steps to describe the future which they prefer. Of course, the winners are those who continue to work until they have achieved their objectives.

In Chapter 13 you will add intuition to your tools of prediction. Intuition used to be thought of as picking up answers from mysterious sources inside and outside us. Today we know where intuition comes from and can actually improve it!

I believe we can alter a likely future by awareness and action to bring about a more preferable future. This is easiest to see in work with young people. Without much life experience, it is difficult for them to predict the result of decisions or nondecisions they make in the present. Based upon their present trajectory we can develop a likely set of scenarios. For example, we can estimate the career opportunities available to a young person given his or her current academic success and interests. Through discussing likely scenarios, the young person may make near-term decisions that would alter a probable future into a more preferred one.

Sometimes there is enough information about an environmental trend to make confident predictions. For example, "more hybrid cars will be produced as a function of energy prices and the desire for conservation." Here are the macro forces are in play, and while we can't change them, we can recognize them as highly likely factors in our future. Predictions do not have to be made on supercomputers. As Yogi Berra said, "you can see a lot just by observing."

CHAPTER 11

The Truth About Statistics, or Why You Need a BS (Bad Statistics) Filter

Round numbers are always false.

SAMUEL JOHNSON

"It ain't so much the things we don't know that get us in trouble," said Artemis Ward, "It's the things we know that ain't so."

Some information arrives in the form of so-called best practices. These are purportedly the inside tips that will deliver improved results. Unfortunately, very few best practices are researched well enough to prove a repeatable cause and effect. When closely examined, many appear to be lucky coincidences that *may* work for you—or make you worse off.

Experts in decision making say we could improve just by using common sense and applying simple statistics we learned years ago. Here is an example: Our friend Bob, a new CEO with only three weeks on the job, asked for our help in evaluating a potential Chief Sales Officer. Sales had been declining. He decided to fire the CSO he inherited, who had been in place less than a year.

"What happened to the guy before the current one?" we asked. The answer surprised us.

"His predecessor lasted only a few months." He explained the five-year declining sales problem and the company's attempts to find a CSO to turn things around.

We calculated that the next CSO would be the seventh in five years. Obviously, this pattern screamed that something was very wrong in this company. Sales was taking the blame, yet it was a good bet there was something else at the root of the problem.

If the CEO applied simple statistics to the pattern, he would have had a big surprise.

What is the probability that a billion-dollar firm could make six consecutive bad hires in this critical position? Let's do the math. Say that as a guideline, as careful as one is in such an important hiring decision, that one in two new hires does not work out. Therefore, the probability is that there's a 50% chance that each of the six past CSOs would have been a bad hire. What are the odds of making two bad hires in a row?

To determine this probability, multiply the probability of each occurrence to calculate the probability that there will be two consecutive bad hires: 50% × 50% = 25% chance.

OK, how about three consecutive bad hires? 50% × 50% × 50% = 12.5%. You can see where we are heading. It is going to be under 2% probability that anyone could hire six experienced, well-recommended, closely interviewed sales executives in a row, and be wrong about each one!

A Short History of Bad Numbers

It seems to be an abiding characteristic of us all to accept too much information at face value. Sometimes we get the information from experts, and it seems highly plausible. However, that does not make it correct. In the example that follows, the incorrect information came from a source no less than Aristotle.

In the late 300s BCE, Aristotle stated that a ten-pound weight would fall to the earth ten times as fast as a one-pound weight. The speed of the fall was proportional to the weight. Legend says that in 1612 Galileo simultaneously dropped a musket ball and a cannonball from Tower of Pisa to prove Aristotle wrong.

Today we may smile when we hear these and other apocryphal beliefs. Yet, even today we want to know how things work. We don't like to believe that things happen randomly. We like to believe the world is orderly and that we can identify causes for what happens. Here are several examples in our own time.

Get a Pet and Become a CEO

Most of us are interested in learning tricks of the trade from those who made it to the top. Here's a suggestion describing one of the more painless ways to make it to the corner office.

"Results of a recent survey of 74 chief executives indicate that there may be a link between childhood pet ownership and future career success. Nearly 94% of the CEOs, all of them employed within Fortune 500 companies, had possessed a dog and cat or both as youngsters."[1] Many of the CEOs believed that pets helped them develop many of the important character traits that helped them get to the top.

This is the sort of news that many mothers may have clipped from the newspapers and sent to their promising children. However, there's nothing to indicate that there's any truth to it whatsoever. This is an example of someone jumping to a conclusion that does not necessarily follow from the facts. This is speculation.

To demonstrate a "link," the author must provide information to back up the assertion. We need to know, for example, what percentage of CEOs with businesses that failed were pet owners? Is there a meaningful difference from those who succeeded? What if we learned that 94% of those sentenced for felonious assault were also pet owners?

Grow Tall; Become a CEO

In researching *Blink,* Malcolm Gladwell surveyed the Fortune 500 to learn something else interesting about CEOs. He found that they are disproportionately tall and that the bigger the company, the taller the average CEO. "In the U.S. population, about 14.5 percent of all men are six feet or over. Among CEOs of Fortune 500 companies, that number is 58 percent. Even more strikingly, in the general American population, 3.9 percent of adult men are 6'2" or taller. Among my CEO sample, 30 percent were 6'2" or taller."[2]

Gladwell also mentions that the overwhelming majority are also white males, so tallness may not be the only link. Does the tallness attribute really say anything about the CEOs, or do we impute some attribute? Is our well-researched prejudice in favor of tall people for leadership positions responsible for this? Does it demonstrate our prejudice against short people?

Does anyone get to be a CEO purely because of his or her competence? I don't know; however, the numbers would be interesting.

I hope the point is emerging how easily we can jump to conclusions before all the facts are in. What's more, proving that something is the cause of something else is a complex task.

Even relationships that appear obvious can fool us. Even by observing apparent cause and effect with our own eyes, we may be deceived. In this next case, we have both our own observation and the testimony of experts. We still become deceived!

Champagne Secret

Once opened, do you think champagne could keep its fizz in the refrigerator overnight? Yes, according to a British magazine *New Scientist*. Here's how.

"Champagne will keep its fizz if the spoon is suspended in the neck of the bottle as long as the spoon does not touch the liquid. Why is this?"[3] The editors performed the experiment with the spoon in the neck but not touching the liquid and learned it worked as promised for 12—even 24 hours. *The claim appeared correct!* Someone then decided upon a blind taste test against champagne that had been stored without the spoon. No one could tell the difference. The point of this story is the illusory demonstration of cause and effect of a spoon to preserving the bubbles in champagne. As a side note, my wife and I corked our unfinished bottle from New Year's Eve and found it just as effervescent six nights later.

How to Test for Cause

A true relationship *will pass* each test (see Table 11.1). How often do we jump to premature judgment? Once we do, as this experiment

TABLE 11.1 Testing for Cause

Steps	Result
1. Every time A (spoon) was present, B (fizz) happened.	Yes.
2. When A was not present, B did not happen.	Not true. Good fizz anyway.
3. B did not happen when other events besides A were present.	Not true. B always happened.
4. The reason B took place when A was present is explainable by some natural law or reasonable explanation.	Not true. There is no reasonable explanation of why a spoon would preserve fizz.

shows, it is easy to confirm what we already believe. This tendency can profoundly affect a career.

Let us observe how this principle of illusory causation undermines a sales management team in the following.

The Illusory Link

Jeff's GM just returned from the company management meeting in Hawaii. Jeff was VP of sales in a Boston telecom firm with three regional managers reporting to him. They were struggling to reach quota and delighted to have a few days out from under their GM, who was showing concern over struggling sales.

In reviewing the meeting, Jeff's GM told him he had learned from the Houston GM that compared to Boston, sales per rep were 50% higher in the Houston office. Jeff was flabbergasted. Perhaps, the GM strongly suggested, Jeff ought to find out what they were doing differently down there.

The implication (premature conclusion) was that the sales management team in Houston was employing some best practices unknown to Jeff's team. Jeff checked out the GM's story. Houston reps were averaging twice the revenue per rep. He had a problem.

What was he doing wrong? What were the managers in Houston doing to inspire those results?

"Boston, We Have a Problem"

Jeff compared everything from funnel management to compensation and could not find any meaningful differences in the sales programs. He tacitly accepted the GM's conclusion that Houston knew how to do something that Boston did not. Perhaps it *was* him.

Jeff was terminated six weeks later. Had he been more aggressive in digging for answers, he might have retained his job. He began with a faulty assumption: the GM's implication that the difference in performance was linked to Boston's sales management program and Jeff's leadership. Perhaps the CEO is correct. However, there is no information to suggest this or any one of a dozen other plausible explanations. Let's dig in.

What Does "Average" Really Mean?

The CEO claimed average sales in Houston per rep were 50% higher than those in Boston. Table 11.2 shows the results of the two teams.

TABLE 11.2 Team Results

	Houston	Boston
Rep #1	600	630
Rep #2	725	755
Rep #3	2200	600
Rep #4	745	710
Rep #5	725	660
Rep #6	—	710
Rep #7	—	605
Rep #8	—	550
	Total 4995	Total 5220
	Mean 999	Mean 652
	Median 725	Median 645
	Mode 725	Mode 710

There are three terms statisticians use to describe the loose term "average":

1. mean
2. median
3. mode

People have been known to select one meaning or another to dramatize their point. It is a very effective device and difficult to blame one who uses it. Always be certain to ask what someone means when he says "average."

Which Average?

Mean takes all the individual sales results, totals them, and divides by the number of reps to get $999,000 for Houston vs. $652,000 in Boston. By this definition Houston's "average" is actually 53% higher.

The *median* figures are middle figures that tell you that half the reps did more and half did less. Houston's median of $725,000 is just a 12% improvement over Boston's $645,000 per rep. On "average," performance of the two teams is much closer by this measurement.

If we used *mode*—the most frequently met number in a series—to compare the teams, the averages would have been closer still with Houston's $725,000 a scant 2% better than Boston's $710,000. The modal average results for Houston and Boston are nearly identical.

Had Jeff done more thorough homework, he would have asked about the range of sales. Note that one rep booked a whopping $2,200,000. This really skewed the "average" (mean). Where did this deviation come from? It was a one-time sale to a Fortune 500 firm moving into Houston. Does it seem strange that no one flagged this aberration?

How did the Houston team do last year? Boston hit its numbers. Was this a one-time fluke? The Houston branch had just five sales reps. This is too small a sample size to which to compare anyone's results. Anything is possible with such a small sample. For example, we know that half the time the coin will land heads, the other half sales. With just five flips, you could get five heads. Is that meaningful?

The better question is how are the other 200 sales reps doing across the United States?

There is no evidence that Houston's success is due to a superior sales management program. Without any causal evidence, Houston results may simply have been random.

Jeff also had a political problem. We know the GM already had concerns about Jeff's performance before the GM meeting. He is already watching Jeff's performance through a developing perception that Jeff is not the sales leader he needs. Therefore, even if Jeff presented strong evidence that Houston was not the norm, it is unlikely the CEO's perception would have changed. In a later chapter, you will learn why perceptions are difficult to reverse. Besides, Jeff's position would be suspect because it would appear self-serving. To be credible, Jeff would need help.

Knowing this, how could Jeff deliver his analysis with greater impact? He needed the help of a neutral third party. Unfortunately, he had neglected to develop a close relationship with the VP of Marketing. Had Jeff and the marketing VP developed a case together, it would have had more impact. As one CEO told us, "I tend to see sales arguing from an emotional standpoint. VPs of Marketing come in with numbers. They have much more credibility with me." We will return to the importance of internal alliances.

Illusory Correlation

The CEO was under an illusory cause-and-effect correlation, mistaking that management was the link to Houston's success and to underperformance in Boston. Jeff let him get away with this thinking error. It's the same type of error that connects pets with business success, that keeps bubbles and spoons in champagne.

One of the rules of the game is that the boss always wins regardless of whether he is right. Jeff couldn't win by proving the boss wrong. He could only have won by providing the information for the boss himself to see that he was wrong. That's when you need all the credibility—and supportive alliances and colleagues—you can create.

Be a thoughtful consumer of numbers, studies, and heuristics. Don't get snookered by accepting numbers that aren't all they seem to be.

As humorist Henry Felson reminded us: Proper treatment of a cold will cure it in seven days, but left to itself, a cold will hang on for about a week.[4]

CHAPTER **12**

The Gullibility Factor

Believe nothing, no matter where you read it, or who said it, no matter if I have said it, unless it agrees with your own reason and your common sense.

BUDDHA

In March 2004, the city council of Aliso Viejo, California, scheduled a council vote to ban Styrofoam cups at city events because the substance DHMO was used in their manufacture. A paralegal researcher discovered this and more about DHMO on a *website (www.dhmo.org)* sponsored by the Environmental Assessment Center. In its notice of the proposed vote, the city fathers explained that DHMO was poised to "threaten human safety and health."

Further research confirmed that because it is cheap, DHMO was commonly used as an industrial solvent despite being found in 95% of cervical cancer tumors. The substance was routinely found in both nuclear power and biological weapons manufacturing plants. They easily dispose of DHMO by dumping it into the environment where it becomes the major component of acid rain. Ingestion of even small amounts of DHMO into human lungs kills thousands each year. Yet it was discovered that the substance runs freely in some Aliso Viejo streets.

Obviously, the scheduled council vote mobilized environmentalists and firms manufacturing Styrofoam cups.

Actually, the council was spoofed. DHMO (dihydrogen monoxide) is simply the chemical name for ordinary water. I tell this fascinating story to show how easily intelligent people can be roped in to run with the herd. The DHMO gag is an easily recalled reminder of how important critical thinking is to our jobs.

We are bombarded daily in our personal and business lives with information that rings with the authenticity of common wisdom and support of experts. (Joseph Stalin was selected as *Time* Magazine's Man of the Year in 1939—and again in 1942.) Some of it is helpful; some, such as the peril of DHMO, is not. This chapter is about best practices and how to evaluate them critically. My aim here is to improve your aim, as it were, so that you make better choices to increase the odds that you will succeed in achieving what you want.

Beyond helpful and unhelpful information, sales managers are also exposed to *mis*information and *dis*information. You rarely get *enough* information, and what you get may be larded with half-truths. Now that you know DHMO is ordinary water, look back and see for yourself that everything you are told about it is technically true. Nevertheless, it is highly misleading.

"How Gullible Are We?"[1]

Simple due diligence would have saved the Aliso Viejo council the national embarrassment it brought upon itself. A simple Internet search would have revealed that the DHMO spoof was an old one repopularized by the science project of a 14-year-old Eagle Rock, Idaho, student named Nathan Zohner. Zohner based his project on a report he downloaded from the Internet that provided factually correct information on DHMO, including this clincher: "For those who have developed a dependency on DHMO, complete withdrawal means certain death."

His project "How Gullible Are We?" won first prize. He reported the results of his survey in which 86% of his 50 science classmates said they would vote to ban the substance. Obviously, Zohner's survey was not a fluke. David Murray of the Statistical Assessment Service believes that there is a high probability of replicating the boy's results with a survey of U.S. Congressmen.

What Are Best Practices?

Adoption of a best practice is a time when some managers demonstrate their gullibility and not their intellectual smarts. A best practice is a "management idea which asserts that there is a technique, method, process, activity, incentive or reward that is more effective at delivering a particular outcome than any other technique, method, process, etc. The idea is that with proper processes, checks, and testing, a project can be rolled out and completed with fewer problems and unforeseen complications."[2] One of the ironic things about best practices is that we often wait until problems arise to implement a practice that would have made sense all along. It makes no sense to wait until sales plunge before announcing: "We must get back to basic blocking and tackling."

As I wrote this book, I was introduced to a friend of a friend writing a business book for another publisher. That author was a former business consultant who made his living by introducing organizations to best practices. After several interesting conversations about writing experiences, our collegiality ended abruptly when I told him that I was writing a chapter for my book about "how best practices could kill you." When his book hit the market, I understood why. His premise and each of his chapters outlined best practices that would allow one to grow one's business from here to the moon or, one presumes, any desirable point in between. Actually, I suggest some best practices in this book, such as thin-slicing, while I remain skeptical of most best practices.

Best practices are not religious tenets. Faith alone supports religious doctrine; best practices should be supported by evidence. Two Stanford professors who study cause-and-effect issues put it bluntly in their book *Hard Facts:* "Too much common management 'wisdom' isn't wise at all—but instead, flawed knowledge based on best practices that are actually poor, incomplete, or outright obsolete."[3]

Tragedy and Best Practices

History is replete with bad best practices, many with pitiful consequences. Take the example of George Washington whose well-regarded physician was summoned to treat the great man's sore throat. As was the best practice of the time, the physician used bloodletting to treat the malady. Draining five pints of blood did nothing to improve the General's health. In fact, it killed him. Unfortunately, for the Father of Our Country, it wasn't until 1836 that Pierre Louis determined that the best practice of bloodletting actually lead to more deaths.[4]

Over 200 years later, many coaches and athletic directors tell their athletes to hydrate themselves before grueling marathons and long cross-country runs. As it turns out, too much water has led to the death of runners during these races.[5]

Thankfully, the risk of best practices are rarely so high. Some are simply irksome.

Take the IT department urging everyone to change passwords every month. It sounds like a reasonable idea, and it was at the time of old, free-standing computers. Today with sophisticated networks, changing passwords monthly doesn't make much sense. With frequent password changes, users tend to write them down in places easily accessible to malicious users, use easily guessed words for simplicity, and take up more system administration time to look up forgotten passwords.[6]

Herding and Best Practices

Robert Prechter, President of Elliot Wave International and developer of a new theory of socionomics, observes that society herds together as it shares prevailing social moods. He says we share collective memes that make us gloomy, optimistic, skeptical, etc. Communications technology spreads and intensifies our social mood. Prechter's ideas become novel as he observes that our social mood is the *cause* rather than the result (effect) of events. In other words, a bull stock market does not cause a positive social mood. Rather, the market is the most easily visible result of our social mood. When we view some business behavior in the past decade through the lens of socionomics, we can spot the genesis of some best practices.

Dotcom Euphoria

We were happy and frisky in the second half of the 1990s. Planning and careful cash management practices were out of favor. Awash with cash, we were undeterred by high burn rates. In one example of our collective insanity, we invested over $100 million in boo.com, and never made a penny. Organic growth was out and mergers and acquisitions were in. The bigger the better, à la the $350 billion ill-fated merger of Time Warner and AOL. In 2007, investors were still wondering what happened to $160 billion in AOL market capitalization, which has disappeared since the day the merger was announced.

Outsourcing, already big, became huge. Attracting "eyeballs" (site visits) and counting click-throughs drove new practices because "this time it was different." Then our mood shifted as we soured on infinite ROIs and the practice of buying companies at multiples of sales that would not be achieved for decades. By mid-2000, the bottom began to drop out, and we ran from NASDAQ stocks. We stopped funding companies whose business plans were based on clicks and not revenue. We sobered, and then sobbed as trillions of dollars evaporated in telecommunications stocks alone.

Our response was to return to common practices of chopping, slicing, and squeezing out more productivity. Profitable growth regained importance. This pushed sales quotas up and the longevity of sales vice presidents down. Their average tenure in Silicon Valley dropped from nineteen to twelve months.

We posed an interesting question to one of our experts. When it's apparent that the herd is in control and you don't feel good about the direction it is running, what can you do? He had an interesting answer. He suggested keeping a low profile during such madness and not actively taking a stand against a popular practice. He simply drags his feet, implementing the practice so slowly that it runs its course before harm is done. "Things usually return to their center point," he says.

Caution: No Silver Bullets for Sales!

Alan Cervasio, vice president for global sales strategy at Marriott Vacation Club International in Orlando, Florida, reminds us that "best practices are a constantly moving target, and there really is no silver bullet."[7] He believes that constant improvement is essential, but does not spend his time looking for canned answers. He keeps his eyes open for new ideas, but relies ultimately upon his own experience and intuition before making changes.

For example, do you need the best people and must you pay the industry's highest salaries for sales managers and salespeople? Not necessarily. It was not high wages that made Southwest Airlines so successful. Former CEO Herb Kelleher claimed his secret to success was, "to drink plenty of good whiskey." This is not a practice recommended for everyone! Southwest had a great strategy and a can-do culture. There are stories of pilots helping baggage handlers load planes to get flights off on time. They delivered what they promised and customers loved it.

IBM's Success Environment

I have a personal story about the power of a company's environment to shape the success of its people. As a salesman at the IBM Corporation, I had a recurring observation about whether it was the people that make an organization great or vice versa. Every time I thought about this, I had the same conclusion. IBM had power to inspire greatness in even average people. Working in a confident environment put extra starch into everyone's white shirts.

IBM practiced what it preached. In particular, there were several principles that inspired me. The first was respect for the individual, the second: the best customer service of any company in the industry, and third: the pursuit of all tasks in a superior manner. The environment was such that I observed our sales managers, even to the top of the house, were guided by these principles. Superior performance was expected and propelled me in tough times such that I never missed qualifying for a 100% Club. In my third year, I achieved the Golden Circle, the top one-half percent of sales representatives. Although my observation is anecdotal, the power of good managers to create great performers is well known.

In their book *Hard Facts,* Jeffrey Pfeiffer and Robert Sutton debunk the correlation of big bucks and team success in a 1999–2002 study of the As and the Yankees. The Yankees paid 300% more than the As for their average player. Yet the performance of both teams was superb. For example, each team made the league playoffs during the study years and won the same number of games in 2002. The Yankees, being the Yankees, did advance twice to the World Series and won it in 2000.

Examine the Evidence

It is difficult to verify cause and effect and know with high probability that if you do this, you'll get that. Often random luck is responsible for results. Sometimes there are additional factors that create success, not the ones claimed by the best practice. For example, say a company created a virtual sales organization moving all employees out of the office and into their homes. The objective was to improve sales productivity by reducing travel time and gaining more face time with customers. Assume that after several months sales results increased.

The meager facts of this example don't make home offices a best practice. There is not enough information to know whether you will achieve the same result. To make a responsible judgment, you need more evidence, even if it is hard to find. What proof do we have that adopting virtual office topology caused the sales spurt? Have others had similar success? Do sales always increase? Or is this result a simple coincidence? Perhaps there were other unreported factors responsible for the sales increase, such as a change in the compensation plan, or a competitor's capacity problem? The following questions will help you discern the viability of a best practice for your organization:

Does the purported best practice have good evidence to support it?

Does the practice address the real problem to be solved?

Can the practice be implemented to work in your organization?

Does the proposed practice agree with your reason, common sense, and intuition?

In summary, as former President Reagan suggested, "trust but verify."

Application to a Forecasting Gap

Let's apply these questions to a common situation, a forecasting gap for the coming year.

You present a bottoms-up view of sales for the new year. Your view falls significantly short of the view that marketing already provided to the CEO. You are maximizing all the resources you have. You expect pushback from marketing and the CEO, who also supports this ambitious stretch plan.

At your meeting with the CEO and Marketing VP, the negotiation starts with an open-ended question "Well, then, what would sales need to have or do to reach this objective?" You know it is impossible to hit their number with the resources you have and tell them so. They anticipated your response. A number of prepared possibilities are now laid upon the table for your adoption.

"Okay, let's say we added five sales reps, at $750,000 production each. That would increase sales by about 10%. Right?"

"What if the ad budget were increased by $50,000? Would that have a 5% increase impact on sales?

"What if we became distributors for the Frammis line? That will add to our top line by, say, 10%?"

"And what if we doubled the amount of training in the budget for next year so that your people became solution-selling experts? Could we wring a 5% increase in sales from that investment?"

Then comes the big fallacy of logic.

"So if we do all of these things, then we could achieve the company's plan for next year of 30% growth. Right?"

Every sales manager wants to contribute his or her part. In fact, we are usually overeager to commit to challenges. We are in sales, after all! At first glance, the solution may appear logical. It addresses the problem of resources and can be implemented here. The overeager sales manager displays his gullibility, succumbs to the pressure, and accepts the risk.

He may have placated his CEO; however, intuitively it does not feel right. Here is where some simple math and careful thinking would help.

First, what is the evidence that each of these off-the-cuff estimates will contribute its stated percent contribution to next year's sales? Even if the math and evidence supported each piece of the solution individually, the question remains whether the pieces of the solution taken individually will add up to a 30% sales increase. They won't. Here's why.

An MIT scientist explained to me that we almost never achieve large improvements by combining many small changes, *even* when each of those small changes has been tested and proven. This is because many of the changes can be related or correlated. Each is not an airtight compartment on its own. There's more. Even if tested, some changes may not produce the same results in your organization.

Finally, each of the considered changes has its own dynamic, and what worked last year could be far less effective in this year's dynamic environment. Think about an email spam filter that was so effective a few months ago and is ineffective today.

The only way to answer the question of how effective the proposed changes will be is to test them together in the coming year. Right now, they are speculative guesses and make a commitment risky. Gain agreement on a level of commitment that you judge is attainable and will not be career limiting.

Exponential Sales Growth

Here is another example of a modest growth proposal—which turns out not to be modest at all. This applies to situations of exponential growth with supposedly correlated outcomes.

A friend tried to sell me a security products distributorship with the idea that I could become part of an exponential growth opportunity by recruiting just two additional salespeople to create my network. The next step is that each of my two people would recruit two more, and each of these would recruit two more. . . . If my network grew thusly each day, by month's end I would become filthy rich because of the laws of network growth.

In applying some college statistics, however, my hopes were dashed. I figured that with each step occurring as proposed, I would have recruited the entire population of the United States within a month! (2 people to the 29th power is 536 million.) There just aren't any silver bullets!

Additional Insights

As a consultant I come across the "next great thing" regularly. Things being rarely what they seem, here are fourteen additional insights from my experience.

1. The culture of one company varies so much from another that the people-factor can torpedo the success of any change. Germans describe this unique force as *leitbilder*. Like an iceberg, a company's *leitbilder* is massed below the surface and invisible. Every important change must address these employee norms, fears, and experience. It is folly to assume that what worked successfully at one company will work as well at another with a different *leitbilder*.

2. Many best practices are actually small-risk changes. They appear attractive when a manager's confidence is low and he has no better ideas to glom on to. There is a felt need to take some action with little risk of failure. However, running a sales contest is no long-term solution for addressing a declining market. When a Hindenburg Omen threatens your viability, there is no time for pussyfooting around. Deliberate action is required.

3. When a company adopts outside practices, its own employees may feel their contributions are not valued. One CEO adopted the practice of rejecting any product innovation that would not

produce $50 million in revenue in its first year. At first, several interesting innovations below the $50 million mark were suggested to test his resolve. After all, it was an extraordinarily high bar. Nevertheless, he batted the ideas back. His insistence on that threshold kept him from hearing some promising ideas that may have paid off handsomely in the future. The lesson of six sigma demonstrates the importance of continuous improvement. Be open to internal sources of incremental improvement and innovation.

4. Motivated employees can create their own best practices. Witness GE's workout program. A workout brings together the people across departments who own the problem. Despite diverse and even competing interests, they are required to work together until they hammer out solutions they agree to implement. Then they present their programs to their managers for comment and approval. GE's success with internal workouts presents a best practice to sales leaders seeking solutions for thorny internal problems. Empower your own people to develop good solutions within your group and as your plenipotentiaries to other departments.

5. Many CEOs, knowing relatively little about sales, often suggest more training as their solution to a sales shortfall. Of course, training is always helpful, but it has never been the universal solution many CEOs believe it is. More training will never overcome a product/market mismatch. Address the root cause of the sales shortfall.

6. The implementation of best practices can hurt productivity by consuming employee hours. Some employees view these consulting interventions as programs of the month. Others become discouraged over the investment of the company's treasure and their time. Further, some become disillusioned with their leader's judgment.

7. Recently a salesperson complained about implementing a CRM system. Charged with inputing the data, she complained about the time, opportunity cost, money, and management's intelligence. The best sales managers anticipate such a reaction and are prepared with both practical solutions for inputing and a compelling presentation of the value of the CRM system to achieving corporate objectives.

8. By emulating a competitor's practices, you will not gain parity. Even if a competitive firm had IBM's sales force practices, it would not achieve sales force parity. By the time you catch on to adopting a competitor's practices, your competitor may be well on to a better practice. You have your own *leitbilder* and differences in capital structure, capacity, locus of market control, and management effectiveness. Your job is to commit to intelligent changes and innovations in your own context.

9. All practice changes incur costs—not just in cash. The cost of organizational focus is just as real. Therefore, it may be wise to experiment first before making large changes. Rather than hire new product specialists for every branch in the country, experiment with the concept in a region first. Yahoo, for example, tests new ideas constantly to gather evidence about the wisdom of a major change.

10. Be straightforward with the organization. If change is implemented with ulterior motives, salespeople will spot the duplicity a mile away. We interviewed a CEO who invested in CRM software with a *sub rosa* agenda. His motive was to neither assist sales nor improve customer service. The investment was primarily to satisfy a supplier whose line provided a certain prestige. The ruse was obvious to the sales force, which knew the supplier's products were a mismatch for their market. The training and tracking time simply saddled them with a make-work system certain to diminish their enthusiasm for management's next great idea. Always be truthful.

11. People appear fickle because they are pragmatic. They want to know what you will do for *them* and could care less about what was done before under your previous employer. People are turned off to hear that secondhand practices will be good for them. A couple of years ago Bill Weld, the former governor of Massachusetts, ran for governor of New York. Promising to do there what he had done here in Massachusetts won him a quick ticket to the sidelines. It is arrogant to think that what made you successful in one environment will make you successful in another!

12. Research confirms the power of managers to create winning sales teams without silver bullets. All that is required, according to Harvard Professor Teresa Amabile, is diligent application of ordinary

management practices. "Leaders must understand how ordinary, seemingly mundane things they do or say carry great influence on workers—so "sweat the small stuff."[8]

13. Another study about key success factors for sales found creativity and ego to be the best indicators of future success. Professor Amabile's work shows hiring a creative genius is no requirement for creativity. Her work demonstrates that if you create the right environment, ordinary people are capable of extraordinary creativity. Focus on the little things to encourage creativity in even average people.

14. Mindfulness is a useful sales management skill. Simply put, it is consciously reviewing every interaction for how successful you were in gaining what you wanted and in anticipating the other's response. Like intuition, one learns most from replaying a situation immediately afterward in your mind with the critical view to evaluate how you might have become more successful in the future with that individual and that situation.

Intuition

The highest reward for a person's toil is not what they get for it, but what they become by it.

JOHN RUSKIN

Your intuition is extraordinarily critical to your success, and you use it almost constantly. Nobel Prize winner Daniel Kahnemann has studied decision making and found intuition to be one of the two broad ways we think. The other is reasoning. Reasoning requires work, while intuition comes to us naturally and effortlessly. Moreover, even in making a complex decision, intuition is always there in the background whether we know it or not.

We drive our cars by intuition, and we respond quickly and easily to questions with the help of our intuition. Kahnemann is convinced that our intuition is highly reliable, but that there are specific times that it causes us trouble. These are the cognitive illusions we described in earlier chapters.

This chapter is about understanding and developing your intuition. Good intuition is an essential tool of successful sales managers. They use their experience to take better aim on a preferred future. As Einstein implies, even geniuses cannot succeed without healthy intuition.

Einstein said, "The only real valuable thing is intuition."[1] His observation suggests a critical difference of sales management from other company functions. There are no well-formed processes or procedures for many sales decisions. Almost everything is situational and requires on the spot application of intuition.

This chapter may change your understanding of intuition. Many people have a mistaken impression that intuition is magic. It is not. Moreover, it is not just plain instinct. Instincts are those things that evolution has hardwired into us and that will work just as well with or without experience. Touching a hot stove will demonstrate instinct. Touch it and you will pull away!

Intuition Is Experience, Not Magic

Intuition is our deep valuable experience in an area that helps us make better decisions and will get us recognized as experts. In basic terms, it is having a gut instinct about something. It can be a vague sense that we have seen this before or that something here isn't quite right. It shines in situations where there are no handy analytical tools. Intuition helps us navigate in the field when we are under time pressure and stress. Great chess players, for example, use their intuition to play well even under artificially heightened pressure.

Spreadsheets or other analytical tools don't help us in the field where we are almost always dealing with incomplete or ambiguous information. Intuition helps us make sense of it. Before we are even conscious of it, our intuition is in play to quickly recognize patterns in the information we have so that we can make quicker decisions. Our intuitive pattern matching may create a sense that something missing or is just not right and requires further examination. As a sales manager, you are constantly making decisions in this environment. As Einstein suggested, intuition is your only way to make some complex decisions. That is why good intuition is essential for you to excel in sales management. Without good intuition, a sales manager would play like Charlie Brown in the cartoon we discussed in the previous chapter.

Experience in Action

Researcher Gary Klein defines intuition as "how we translate our experience into action."[2] Wind and Crook say "Intuition is different from either insight or instinct in that it is generally based upon a deep experience in a certain area."[3] Some think intuition is paranormal reception of information.

My first experience with intuition occurred with the best-selling author and MIT researcher Dr. Peter Senge. I enrolled in his program on systems thinking. During one of the exercises, we conducted an experiment on intuition. He wanted to observe the power of our group mind to see if it could draw accurate insights from minimal information.

To demonstrate this, he said only the name "Dana Meadows." He asked us to say what came to mind about this name. She has since died but, at that time, none of us had ever heard of this young Dartmouth professor who would become a noted environmentalist. We concentrated on her name, listening intently to the words each member used to describe her. After three times around, we had about a dozen pieces of information. Senge then told us that she was a friend of his and that our descriptions of her were accurate.

Intuition Is Mainstream

I have tried but have never been able to duplicate that experience reliably. However, I did begin a study of intuition. I think intuition is having a feeling or a knowing that comes from our internal wisdom and experience. It also saves us a lot of time! Without it, we would have to reason through all our decisions.

Reason is the scientific method: We identify a problem, examine the key elements, determine alternatives, calculate payoffs, develop an action plan, execute, and follow up. Herbert Simon, a 1978 Nobel Prize winner, explained that it is nearly impossible in making any complex decision to gather and analyze all the facts. There are so many combinations and permutations that our minds simply cannot handle them all to make a truly analytical decision. Instead, Simon believes that we actually use our intuition to arrive at decisions. Over the years, our brains construct many useful mental models to simplify life by speeding up our decisions. Intuition calls upon these models unconsciously. Some people allow their intuition to provide an initial answer, and then they check it with analysis.

The scientific view of intuition has changed with some good research over the last few years. Work by Daniel Kahnemann, Robin Hogarth, and Gary Klein looks at intuition as a tool for decision makers at all levels that is reliable and gets better with work.[4] How do we improve intuition?

Saving Luna!

A few days ago, my daughter Kathryn came home from school, dumped her backpack in the middle of the floor, dropped her coat, and crawled over to play with Luna our dog. Suddenly she screamed, "Daddy, look at Luna!"

Our English Setter looked like a Sharpei. Her eyes were swollen shut, and her jowls had ballooned enormously. Just 45 minutes earlier, she appeared normal when she returned from her run. My intuition said that she had eaten poison. We called the vet to advise him of our emergency.

Dr. Hardy coaxed her out of her crate onto his examining table. He asked a couple of questions, observed and felt Luna for several minutes, took her temperature, and gave her two shots of antihistamine.

He concluded that Luna was not poisoned. "It is more likely," he said, "that Luna had been bitten in the face by a spider or stung by a bee." He asked us to call him in one hour and again in the morning to update him on Luna's condition. He provided the telephone number and address of an emergency animal hospital should his diagnosis have been wrong. All of this took less than 15 minutes and required no laboratory tests. All that was required was my check for $129.

I called Dr. Hardy in an hour and told him that the swelling was only slightly improved. By morning, he was delighted to hear that Luna was completely back to normal.

Expertise Is Not Transferable

The story perfectly illustrates several aspects of intuition. First, it demonstrates that my own intuition in the field of veterinary science is worthless. Recall that intuition develops from deep experience in a particular area. My experience in sales management does not necessarily provide reliable intuition in another discipline.

Luna may have had an expensive bee sting, but a less intuitive doctor may have ordered up laboratory tests and a night in the hospital for observation. My sister-in-law just had an $800 overnight for her dog with no result.

Feedback Is Essential to Learn Intuition

Now here is a particularly important point to note. Dr. Hardy asked for and received feedback that confirmed his diagnosis and his intuition. With feedback, Dr. Hardy strengthened his intuition with experience he knew was valid.

Intuition such as Dr. Hardy displayed can't be taught or communicated in a mass email. It builds through awareness and valid experience. Here is the next big point: Our brain collects knowledge for our intuition, but does not know whether the knowledge is valid or invalid unless we tell it. The following illustration makes this point.

"Wicked" Intuition

A cocktail waitress was told that better-dressed people are bigger tippers. Whenever the bar gets busy, she continues to provide the best service for those she believes will tip best. The other patrons received less attention. As a rule, her intuition pays off, for the best-dressed people show themselves to be the better tippers.

This is an example of what scientists call "wicked" intuition because we get the feedback without any proof to know if it is valid. She really does not know what would happen if she accorded the same excellent service to those who were not well dressed. Her intuition could be completely wrong, even as she continually reinforces it. Her livelihood could be based upon the rigorous application of bogus information!

Fortunately, you can train your intuition. The United States military uses exercises to improve intuition in its field personnel. Commanders make life and death decisions and cannot chance having relied on "wicked" intuition. Training assures that people develop intuition from valid experience.

Improve Your Intuition

We pick up experience by living. However, that doesn't make us experts. We really do need conscious practice to make significant improvements in our intuition. An easy first step is to be more aware in situations where you are consciously developing your expertise.

The great management guru Peter Drucker had a formal method of developing his own judgment. When he made an important decision, he wrote down what he expected to occur and the benefits he thought would accrue from his decision. He looked back even after ten or fifteen years to check himself and improve upon his intuition by examining his decision and considering what he missed and might have done differently. Imagine if we practiced this review and assessment in our lives. Do you think we would experience a different life?

"Rounds" for Team Intuition

My branch sold to the medical industry. We implemented a process to improve sales we called "rounds." We assembled our eight managers from sales, systems, and operations. Our patient—we had three to four a month—was the salesperson. Just as in medical rounds, we collaborated with the patient and each other to produce the best thinking of the team for the situation before us.

Each session was limited to one hour. In order to have some commonality for everyone involved, the salesperson began the session with the briefing based upon a military process called "Estimate of the Situation." This was a process developed for military field commanders to identify, consider, and decide upon action for a field situation.

Sharing Intuition

The sales rep briefed the team on the "factors" of the situation. These factors dictated the outcome. For example, "We have no current business with this hospital," is an important factor. Then, the question was what to do about it. This is where we shared and grew our intuition.

All ideas were welcome. In the animated discussions of these ideas, sales and non-sales managers considered and criticized ideas on the table. As you would expect, the outcomes were often unpredictable yet highly valuable for learning and for creating the account strategy. Those less versed in sales gained an appreciation for tactics required in the field. Sales gained an appreciation of internal issues. Often non-sales managers shared new ideas and developed creative ways by which they could help the sales strategies succeed.

After discussion, we laid out alternative strategies, selected the best one, and created a plan. The salesperson gained on-the-spot commitments from others involved. Finally, we discussed a contingency plan in the event our chosen play became unworkable. We recorded commitments for accountability. Weeks or months later, we looked back to learn from our decisions.

CSI: Seeing the Invisible

How else does an expert sales manager use intuition to help her team succeed? Intuition enables us quickly to grasp insights unseen by others. She instantly and unconsciously factors in nuances that her less experienced salesperson could not see. Intuition expert Gary Klein says, "Experts perceive a situation as the patterns and relationships that grew out of the past and will grow into the future, not just the cues that exist at the moment." [5]

On an episode of the hit TV series *CSI*, Grissom, the CSI unit manager, provided a good example of this. He is with the husband of a kidnapped wife at their home. Grissom is repeatedly playing tape-recorded ransom demand and listening intently to the limited information. His intuition is speaking to him. With frayed nerves, the husband angrily asks why he keeps playing it back. Grissom replies that he has found an important clue in what he does *not* hear. He finds the absence of background noise unusual, a clue that the less experienced ears of others missed altogether. Like Grissom, successful sales managers evaluate patterns of information for their presence and their absence.

Intuition Is Knowing What Will Happen

After spotting a pattern, a successful manager runs through mental simulations using his intuition to judge the way a situation may pan out.

Mrs. Whitney was my daughter Emily's second-grade teacher. She had thirty years experience in her job. When we asked questions about Emily's progress at our first review, she easily described the Emily we would all see at the end of the school year. We felt confidence in her prediction, for she had evaluated many children and received thirty years of valid feedback on her assessments of them. Likewise, a good sales manager can run a mental simulation of how a deal is likely to play out. He has been there and he has been there successfully. This separates the experts from the guessers.

Test Your Intuition

Good managers spot patterns and themes from their experience. Usually, their first impression is correct. They run a mental simulation to check it out. Below I have developed three cases to test your intuition. At the end, I have described the actual outcome of the situation. However, other outcomes could have just as easily occurred. Read the cases through, make some notes based upon what your intuition is telling you, and then analyze the case to see what you have learned.

- *Sales management challenge 1.* Your CEO completes an analysis of the sales force's proposal to closed order ratio. "We could be back on track with just a 15% improvement of this number," he observes. He's heard sales complaints from the field that not all the company's departments do all they can to help sales close orders. New sales typically take six months to close. The CEO decides to create a bonus for all department heads to encourage full company integration to improve the order close rate by 15%. What will happen?

- *Sales management challenge 2.* You are under relentless pressure from your CEO and the head of service because your sales forecasts are erratic. A couple of orders one way or another can wildly skew your prediction. You consider ways to improve the forecast and decide to block out an extra day each month for closer review of the field's forecast. You and your staff are currently spending two days a month creating the forecast. How well will this additional effort pay off for you?

- *Sales management challenge 3.* Your top sales reps appear to deliver far more productivity from their territories than others of the same size and profile managed by less successful performers. You need to create some new territories to enlarge the sales force. You wonder if you should take some territory from the top performers or slice off pieces of underperforming territories for the new reps. Where are you most likely to find fertile territory for new reps?

Now, think about the following predictions for what will happen in each situation. See if you agree on the following facts-in-the-future™.

Discussion of Answers

- *Sales challenge 1.* Great idea to get skin in the game for everyone and support the sales effort more visibly. The perceptive sales manager knows that you get what you reward. Unfortunately, what sales needs is more revenue, not a higher rate of proposal wins per se. With a six-month average sale cycle, the bonus is unlikely to create any sustained support because rewards are so distant and therefore almost meaningless. Of course, the sales executive can delay declaring proposals "lost." That will improve their win rate percentage while fattening the "pending" category. To do this would make the manager a visible example of poor ethical practice. If the CEO discovered the ruse, the sales manager's job would be in jeopardy.

- *Sales challenge 2.* Read the chapter on sales forecasting. In some companies, one of several forecasting techniques can reliably compute product sales. Here, however, where relatively few orders dramatically skew your predictions, you will be worse off taking more time to do a task that has such low odds (<25%) of success. The more time you spend with this Sisyphean task, the less time you and your staff have to work on opportunities with better odds of success. Sit down with the service manager and explain why there are variances in the forecasted vs. actual results. Offer to use a statistical method if he is dissatisfied with your current best effort. Then let the CEO know what you've agreed upon.

- *Sales challenge 3.* If you have competent but average performers, the odds are that they are working their territory opportunities more completely than the top performers. However, they are not delivering all they could. In contrast, many top performers develop a smaller number of high performing accounts and mine them. They pay less attention to lower potential accounts. Some may never receive a call. Therefore, you can build the new territories with accounts from both existing territories.

No doubt, predicaments such as these confront you regularly. Often they arise from others in the company who are well intended, but who do not understand how the sales mind works. There are second-level consequences of every action.

CHAPTER 14

How Much Information Is Enough?

Minds are like parachutes. They only function when they are open.

THOMAS DEWAR

In *Blink*, Malcolm Gladwell describes how quickly our brains work to draw conclusions—even in the blink of an eye, hence his title. To demonstrate his point, he reviews the findings of researchers who work with married couples. The researchers look for several indicators, such as a trace of disdain in one partner's voice, and so predict the future of the marriage with high accuracy. When non-experts review the same videotapes, they cannot predict with such accuracy. Like these marriage experts, successful sales managers require relatively little information to tap their own intuitive reservoirs and make reasonably accurate predictions.

You will recall thin-slicing of RFPs from Chapter 4 as a similar process you can use to make certain decisions quickly, and with relatively little information. In this chapter we will talk more about the subject of how much information is required to make good decisions.

Spam Slicing

Are you one of those people who can go through a full mailbox of email and nearly instantaneously separate the valid mail from the spam? If so, you are applying thin-slicing. You may look for a few key variables or patterns, such as who sent the mail. Perhaps you run a mental checklist: Is it something you requested? Are there any past patterns that you recognize as junk mail?

Alternatively, you could open and study each piece of mail before acting upon it. Depending upon your intuition-powered thin-slicing prowess, you will probably tend toward the rapid review end of the continuum. Likewise, successful sales managers who know what to look for make routine decisions faster than those less expert.

Information: Less Is Often More

It seems counterintuitive; however, it is a myth that you cannot have too much information. In fact, having too much information actually increases your risk of making a bad decision!

I have never found a sales manager who in retrospect regretted firing a poor performer. What managers usually regret is not taking action sooner. Managers who tell me, "I decided (I had enough information) to terminate the poor performer, but delayed taking action for another ninety days to be sure." When action is called for, delay is not a risk-reducing tactic. When it is clear that a person is in the wrong job, it is our job to make the change expeditiously.

The following research underscores the sufficiency of just the right amount of information, and how having too much information can cause us to doubt a good decision already made.

The study assigned each of three psychiatrists a different patient. Each one received sketchy but sufficient key information from which to make a valid diagnosis. Then, all received additional information and had the opportunity to change their diagnoses. Finally, all received a third round of information about the same patients and had a final opportunity to review their diagnoses. At each phase of the study, the psychiatrists altered their diagnoses based upon the additional information. What was the effect of more information?

The study demonstrated that the psychiatrists made their best diagnoses with the first sketchy but essential facts. Having more information distracted them and made them question their first clinical impressions. More information actually decreased the accuracy of their diagnoses. These professional, highly trained physicians demonstrate the principle that just the right amount of information is all that is required to make a reasonable decision.

A Lesson Learned from Betting on Horses[1]

In an unclassified CIA publication, we found another interesting experiment that addresses the subject of information management. This is a highly relevant analog because both CIA analysts and sales managers work with incomplete, ambiguous, and often misleading information. Both must sort it, identify key variables, and make decisions, which are often for high stakes.

In this study, experienced handicappers (horseracing aficionados) were shown a list of eighty-eight variables typically found on past performance charts. These included percentage of wins, weight, etc. The handicappers were asked to pick the five most important variables to know in order to pick the winning horse. Then, they picked the top ten, twenty, and forty variables.

Next, the handicappers received a list of the last forty races and were asked to pick the first five finishers using information on their five key variables. Then they picked the race results three more times with ten, twenty, and forty variables. Figure 14.1 displays a fascinating result.

On average, accuracy was the same no matter how much information the handicappers had. Selecting first-place finishers was as good with their five key pieces of information as with forty pieces. In the first round, confidence in their selections was roughly equivalent to their accuracy. Notice, however, that their confidence grew to overconfidence with each new batch of information.

Many other studies produce similar findings linking confidence, accuracy, and amount of information. Confidence grows with more information, but confidence in one's judgment is completely unrelated to whether the judgment is right or wrong. More information

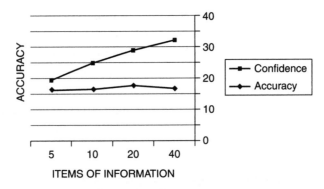

FIGURE 14.1 More information, less accuracy.

makes us solidify our initial judgment, as our antennae are up for information that confirms our position. The more we dig in, the easier it is to disregard disconfirming information. This is human nature.

Sometimes, a single piece of information is all that's required. Think about how you use information, and how much you require. Is information a comfort food that delays decisions while more is gathered?

CHAPTER 15

Mind Games

A man hears what he wants to hear and disregards the rest.

Simon & Garfunkel

Sales management is about making decisions under uncertainty. In this chapter we will see some additional ways to improve how we make decisions and also view an amusing side of ourselves.

Do we always make the best decisions for ourselves? Hardly. In fact, we often make stupid decisions contrary to our own self-interest without even being aware of it. In other words, we are not the cool, rational thinkers we perceive ourselves to be. In the purpose of this chapter is to explain why we do this to ourselves and how we might do less of it in the future.

Most of our faulty decisions are not bad due to some limitation in our ability. Rather, our brains get hijacked by perception, context, and faulty reasoning. This results in errors in both judgment and reasoning, and we are never even aware of them.

Heuristics are guidelines and shortcuts we all use to save ourselves time. For example, when foraging in the refrigerator, if something smells unusual, a rule jumps to mind: If it smells bad, don't eat it. This is a heuristic, a mental shortcut we use automatically and effortlessly to navigate the world. Without these heuristics, we would have to stop and think through even the simplest decisions with a conscious effort.

According to Kahnemann,[1] it is our intuition that guides our minds to employ the proper heuristic for the situation. Most of the time our intuition is fine. However, scientists have cataloged common biases that affect us when we *acquire information, process information,* and *select our response.*

As sales managers, this is important to understand, particularly since we receive information and make most decisions under ambiguity. Ambiguous information plus the likelihood of built-in bias are a recipe for bad decisions. This is when our tried-and-true heuristics hijack our cool, rational thinking.

Kahnemann is not talking about our emotions derailing us. He's talking about us when we believe we are making careful, considered decisions—when we are actually making stupid decisions.

The Availability Heuristic

For example, if we closed a big order the day before we participate in a planning session for the coming year, we are likely to be planning from a positive, optimistic context. Context is everything, because it can distort our view of events associated with our activity.

As we participate in this planning session, we do so with this easy availability of a recent event, namely our big sale. Unaware of the effect of this positive recall, we are more likely now to color next year's results with more confidence and probability than had we lost a large deal the day before.

Remember: The opportunity that actually exists is independent of how you feel about it! This is why context has a lot to do decision making.

There is a similar illusion we fall prey to—the so-called the "man who" fallacy. It is a version of the power of information that is easy to recall because of it is recent or unusual. It could goes like this: "I met another manager in the class who said his company pays 100% of the commission up front and that even so, the reps still remain involved in the implementation." When something sticks to you like this, it can overcome a long history facts to the contrary!

Why? The example is concrete and therefore usually outweighs abstract data, even when this data is more valid. Be attentive to the power of information you collect from firsthand experience. It is likely that this is less representative than a more thorough consideration of available data.

Sales managers tend to jump to conclusions based upon information acquired early in a problem-solving process. Once they do this, they are less open to new information later in the process. Once a point of view is established, managers unconsciously tend to disregard information inconsistent with their established perspective. The advice here is to restrain yourself from jumping to premature conclusions. That way you will be more able to weigh information presented later in the process.

Processing Biases

Once managers form their opinions, those opinions are very difficult to change. They tend to discount information contrary to their opinions. The advice for overcoming this is the same as that above for jumping to premature conclusions.

Sales managers often revert to their tried and true ways. They stick to what they know and have used before, even when it does not fit the current situation. For more about this, see Chapter 18, Evolution in Sales Management.

Stupidity and Probability

Another common fallacy with managers is the conjunction fallacy. The thinking is that if we do one thing, another thing will result. Sometimes applying simple rules of mathematics can improve our decisions. Let us look again at an outrageous but true application of this principle.

The fallacy in this example is that firing the sales manager and bringing in a new one will improve results. In this company, nine new sales vice presidents were hired in seven years, and sales continued to decline. Some simple math demonstrates that something else is going on here. Whatever the problem is, the math says it is not sales management.

Hiring a new Sales VP is important business and done with care. Even so, say there is a only 50/50 chance that a CEO will make the correct hiring decision. What are the odds of making a bad hire twice in a row? As we previously computed, only 13%. Three consecutive bad Sales VP hires? 7%.

We said this is an example of the conjunction fallacy. It's reminiscent of the old adage that flogging will continue until morale improves. No one appears to be aware of the illusion employed here.

Of course, with all the hiring and firing, the CEO lessens his or her chance of success even with a great hire. This is because of the turmoil, turnover, and time to build back to normalcy with each passing régime. Customers become frustrated and must be resold. The reps and line managers must learn new dance steps from each new leader. Competitors gain share. Focus and time are lost. Yet this can be another part of the fallacy unseen by a CEO operating from the illusion of when sales are down, get a new sales manager.

Lonely at the Top

As sales executive, life can get lonely because there's no one to confide in. CEOs have the same problem. Sometimes in sales management, we must bear up under enormous stress and pain for long periods. Perhaps we have missed the forecast or come out of a quarter without making a number. At times like these, it is common suffer a drop in self-esteem. Sales is highly visible and everyone knows when things aren't going well.

These are times that we must be especially aware that we do not slip into a self-fulfilling downward spiral. As the British say, we must keep a stiff upper lip. This is easier to say than do. However, if you can put yourself into the context to understand that similar situations arise predictably, you can have the presence of mind to ride out the tough time when if feels like all the odds break against you.

Neuroscientists Eisenberger and Lieberman observed that you feel personal or social pain the same way the brain feels real pain.[2] Their 2004 study observed participants in a three-way computer game. Each participant believed he was playing against two other players when in reality he was playing against a computer. Shortly after the game began, the computer took over and played keep away from the human participant. The human player was cut out of the game and ostracized.

They recorded the subjects' brain activity and saw that it stimulated the cortex just as real pain does. Now this may be a strange way to make a point about life as a sales executive. However, when you are on your own in the midst of trouble, the mind can play the same tricks as it did on the participants in this experiment. You can take things personally and get so close to the detail that it may appear overwhelming despite your best efforts. The trick is to change your context. It is just a game.

I do not know if knowing this arcane fact will help you bear up under pain any better. It is best to keep your own counsel, and perhaps this insight helps to do that. People have their own problems. Yours can be an imposition or even leave you vulnerable as you display weakness.

A CEO's Advice

One CEO asked that we underscore this point to our readers. Appearing downcast, his sales vice president approached him to share a personal concern. He had a successful first year as sales VP. Many of the salespeople achieved rewards and recognition for their sales success. Nevertheless, the sales VP was feeling low because he personally had not received much validating recognition for his role in all of this. The VP was looking for a shoulder to cry on and a pat on the head from the CEO. The CEO saw this as a deficit, believing that a good sales manager subordinates his own ego to needs of his salespeople. He should be a giver, not a "needer."

Public Stress

Sales management is a highly visible leadership position and is prone to stress. Scholar Roy Baumeister[3] studied the effects of stress on our public face when things seem to be going terribly wrong.

When sales are down, the sales executive's situation is highly public and stressful. If results do not improve, Baumeister says there will be perceptible cracks in the person's composure. Apparently, there is only a limited reservoir of emotional control to draw on. Calm under public stress is like a muscle most do not use often and therefore do not build.

Try as one might to bear up, it is no surprise that prolonged stress burns through the reserve of coolness. Indeed, after even a single major publicly stressful event, one's ability to keep up appearances by overriding negative emotions declines rapidly.

Perhaps you have reported a surprising and highly disappointing result to the Board of Directors. Tough questions were hurled, and you bruised your composure badly and your career seriously.

Baumeister found that with such emotional distress you would have a tendency to make up for such a blow to your pride by taking uncharacteristic steps to right your reputation.

You might abandon your earlier plan and start to go for broke with high-risk, high-payoff situations to climb your way out of your emotional hole. Perhaps you will reorganize the sales force or mandate a doubling of work in the sales pipeline.

As you become more obsessed with getting back to at least even, your judgment could become negatively affected in other ways. You might pour resources and great hope into a major opportunity with a lousy fit for the company. You may make commitments for results that are unrealistic. You could become short-term oriented to a fault.

Perhaps you were always the person who felt that mandating activity quotas is not an effective way to lead a sales organization, but now find yourself setting unrealistic funnel activity metrics for your organization. Your poorly controlled behavior becomes an accelerating downward spiral. You may reach the stage of clinical depression. If you ever identify with this scenario, it is well to seek advice and help outside your company.

Drowning by Hanging onto an Anchor

The CEO asked the senior management team to prepare a bottom-up revenue plan for the coming year. After considering the market, historical growth, and their internal capability, they projected a stretch growth rate of 6%. When they presented their recommendation to the CEO, he only half-heard them. "I had been thinking of something more like 20%," he said.

The CEO had nothing more than a personal desire to grow by 20%, a number he had simply plucked from thin air. Without any change to the existing structure, such as adding additional salespeople or new products, the senior team reworked their numbers to goose them to CEO's personal growth number. The CEO was now happy with the new projection.

In doing as he was told, the sales vice president avoided a conflict with the CEO over a more realistic forecast. He assumed the CEO had his mind made up and, as they say on *Star Trek,* "resistance is futile." He should have known that he would pay for this foolishness now or later. Later is always easier, so he succumbed to pressure to produce a number he could not make.

Results in the first month of the new year were well below the artificially high forecast. The sales executive was terminated a month later. We do not know all the reasons for the CEO's decision. In retrospect, by caving in to the CEO's number, the VP had essentially signed his own death warrant.

The CEO had taken the new forecast to the board and recommended approval. The CEO apparently soon realized the foolishness of his own optimism. By terminating the sales VP, he may have tried to disassociate himself early and decisively with the forecast. This may have provided the cover he needed to rejigger his numbers.

You Take It, You Own It

The rules of the jungle mandate that when you agree to a number, you own it. What should the sales executive have done? First, knowing it would appear to be self-serving if he alone protested to the CEO that the number could not be met, he should have created an alliance at least with the marketing VP. It will be much harder for the CEO to deny evidence presented by these senior officers together.

In most cases, the marketing VP has access to and has more time to assemble the facts and figures of a case than sales. Sales is typically strong presenting a solid logical case. The two together are synergistic and present a strong show of position.

If the CEO continued to demand 20% growth, the sales executive should be prepared with a backup plan. He could ask for the additional resources to achieve the goal. These might include hiring an additional sales team, growing the territory, expanding the product line, or some other rational approach upon which the mandated growth could be built. Then at least, the sales executive is on record with a plan to achieve the CEOs mandate.

No one really knows exactly why anchoring is such a powerful tool of influence. To illustrate it, I am referring back to the CEO who demanded 20% growth. Let us assume he turned down the sales VP's request for more reps, saying he thought the average assigned sales quota was too low and that it ought to be $900,000.

The concept is called anchoring because the number used as a starting point serves to anchor the analysis that follows it by keeping the final estimate closer to the anchor point then it would otherwise be. The CEO's $900,000 is the anchor. Had the senior team known this when it began its analysis of revenue for the coming year, the research says they would have worked to make the growth rate far closer to the 20% than the 6% that they calculated independently. Whereas in the first case, their anchor point may have been actual growth of the previous year, in the second case, with the anchor set by the CEO, they would have achieved a different result.

Scientists have shown that even when subjects are well aware of the psychological influence of anchoring, they still cannot overcome it. This simple classroom experiment illustrates the point. In a classroom, students were asked to estimate the percentage of United Nations member countries located in Africa. Half the class received a low percentage number (10%) and was asked to adjust it after they thought about the problem. On average, this group adjusted the anchor to 25%. The other half of the class began with an anchor of 65%. Its average answer was 45%. The correct answer was 14%. You can see the power of anchoring having significant effect on their answers, particularly since none of the final answers were even close to the correct result.

Overconfidence

Anchoring and overconfidence are biases for most of us even when we are aware of them. Even when experimenters explained the concept of cognitive bias to their subjects and warned them to compensate for it, the subjects were still unable to do so.

In other experiments, even when participants have been told to provide their answer as a range between two numbers so that they were 98% confident in their answer, still 40 to 50% of the time the actual answer fell outside their range![4] It is as if the CEO says, "Give me a range for your forecast between two numbers so that you are certain the actual sales result will be in this range." Half the time we still miss! Sales people are also highly susceptible to a market basket of outside influences and inside biases; the following chapter provides examples the author observed in a single selling situation.

CHAPTER 16

Walk a Mile in the CFO's Shoes

In prosperity our friends know us; in adversity we know our friends.

CHURTON COLLINS

Peter Clarke had checked in at the Southampton Princess less than 30 minutes earlier. He had already jumped into his swimsuit and was winding his way down the steep hill in the hotel shuttle toward the pink sandy beach. It was 80°, and the sea was the same striking blue green that he remembered. Today was the first day of his Golden Oval recognition trip for Raleigh Papers' sales force. Even better, as vice president of sales he was the man in charge of it all.

In a few hours at the opening banquet, he would welcome the company's top salespeople and their significant others. Sales were up 42%, even if profits were not quite where they should be. "Still," he thought, "the year's results were spectacular."

The small bus glided to a stop at the beach. Within minutes, he was stretched out flat on his toweled lounge chair at the hotel's private cove where he knew the water would be as warm as the air. He wondered how anything could be more nearly perfect, and yet a thought he could not shake returned his mind to the senior staff meeting a week before. Culminating several discussions, the CFO announced the program called Large Green.

165

He had an ominous feeling that something more serious than he realized lurked below the surface. Despite all the great sales production, the CFO had been relentlessly critical of Sales all year long. She complained about rebates. She complained that Sales had missed its new days sales outstanding (DSO) metric every month. At staff meetings, she and the Operations VP complained regularly that sales forecasts from every region were uniformly untrustworthy. He perceived they were using Sales as a convenient scapegoat for their own bad forecasts.

He had fought the Finance department's purchase of Large Green all the way. The CFO argued for "transparency" in the company's collection effort. Finance claimed Credit and Collections required a better view into the sales force pipeline and cash forecasting activity.

Peter and his sales managers felt this was an unnecessary administrative burden for the sales force, as busy as it was, since it was impossible to predict collections and sales cash receipts with the accuracy that Finance demanded. They believed the new system was just more administrative work that would take away from the sales effort.

He remembered in the staff meeting hoping that the CEO would be persuaded by his argument about another unnecessary information burden on Sales. However, the CEO never said a word.

Where Does the CEO Stand?

This troubled him. It seemed clear the CEO supported Finance's position. It dawned on him that there must have been some side conversations between the CFO and CEO about the need to keep a closer eye on Sales.

Now, the light lapping of the warm waves on the sand and the warmth of the sun pushed him into a delightful snooze.

The CFO's Viewpoint

Raleigh Paper Company was in an enviable position. Product demand had been so high that the company sold everything it could produce, not just in the United States, but also all over the world.

Sales grew a record 42%, but net income increased only 58%. With this sales volume, the CFO projected net income and cash flow figures that should have been much better, *several hundred percent better*.

In the opinion of the Finance department, the problem had been in sales. As the CFO presented her case to the CEO, she cited three areas where Sales crushed profits.

1. **Poor sales forecasts.** Because of production shortages, salespeople were forecasting sales several months before they actually occurred. To protect their customers, they needlessly scheduled carloads of paper to sit in warehouses for months before they were required. In order to meet sales demand for other customers, production had to import paper from the company's South American plants, another needless expense.

2. **Customer favoritism.** Although the company sold to all customers at an established to list price, some customers received regular rebates and other special attention. The Finance department began tracking these rebates and asking Sales why they were necessary. The typical response was that Sales was building a long-term relationship and had selected that particular customer as the emerging market leader. When Finance followed up several months later about a rebate to a competitor of that customer, Sales simply said this was another customer being groomed just in case conditions changed.

   The CFO didn't bother inquiring about the customer ski trip junket to Italy, although everyone in the company knew about it.

3. **Slow collections.** It was Sales' responsibility to negotiate payment terms for every sale and to follow up on collection when customers deviated from these agreements. Sales submitted a monthly cash forecast of anticipated payments. Raleigh Papers' Treasury department relied heavily on these forecasts in order to manage the company's cash requirements. Unfortunately for Treasury, Sales was notoriously short in its cash forecasts. This caused last-minute negotiations for the company's cash needs at higher rates. Finance regularly monitored the company's DSO

(days sales outstanding) and followed up all forecast deviations monthly with the responsible sales manager.

Sales Takes No Action

The CFO met with Peter Clarke several times to make him aware that his managers and sales reps were costing the company millions in unnecessary expenses. The CFO then reported to her managers that the issues had been addressed with the sales vice president. In all honesty, she had to share with them her opinion that Sales did not understand the cost of its poor cooperation.

Some Finance team members wondered aloud why the company even needed a sales team. After all, customers were pressuring Raleigh for product. It didn't need a costly sales department to sell products that sold themselves.

Increasingly, the CEO pressured Finance and Production to improve their own poor forecasts. Of course, these forecasts were based 100% on information from Sales.

Peter Clarke and his crew may have been having a great sales year, but they were making determined enemies out of Production and Finance. Managing the sales force was quickly becoming a major task of Finance. Yet Finance appeared to make scant progress with all its effort to educate Sales about the effect of its actions to improve results.

Classic Goof

One particular anecdote about Clarke's team became a classic around the company: The Boston branch had a high-visibility customer with over $6 million in receivables outstanding over 60 days. On the last day of the month, the customer personally delivered the check to the branch manager, who then called the CFO to report that he had the check in hand. Unfortunately for everyone, in order to be credited payments had to be received at the company's lockbox by 9 AM on the last day of the month. The branch manager called to announce "mission accomplished" at 1 PM, four hours too late to hit the books that month. This was proof positive that Sales was not educating its own personnel nor managing its customers effectively.

From Finance's point of view, Sales was an untrustworthy and inept team member. Not only was Sales incompetent, but Sales also caused the company's Finance department to appear the same way.

It was for self-defense that the financial management team came up with the idea of buying the Large Green software package. Months ago, they had begun making their case for Sales ineptitude to the CEO and the need for Large Green.

Yes, Peter Clarke and his team had increased sales this year, but at a very dear price.

CHAPTER 17

The Brain of a Sales Manager

If A equals success, then the formula is A equals X plus Y plus Z,
with X being work, Y play, and Z keeping your mouth shut.

ALBERT EINSTEIN

The brain of your average sales executive (and of everyone else) is an astonishingly complex organ. Nobel Prize winner Gerald Edelman observed that if we started counting all the synapses in the human brain at one per second it would take us more than 32 million years. All this complexity weighs about three pounds and is only a bit larger than a grapefruit.

There are three layers of function in our brains. At the center and atop the spinal cord is our most primitive brain. This area controls basic survival skills like breathing and eating. Reptiles and fish have brains that perform these functions.

Wrapped around this layer is the limbic system, which is common to mammals. It contains our thalamus, amygdala, and hippocampus. These components house our emotions such as fear, the sense of contentment, and aggression. The largest and most sophisticated component is the cortex. Other mammals have smaller cortexes. The great size of the human cortex, specifically the prefrontal and frontal lobes, is what makes us human. Hearing and sight are controlled here as are all our high-level thinking processes.

In the last few years, neuroscience has changed much of the thinking about our brains, skills, and personal growth potential. Research dispels some old wives' tales and provides new pathways to grow. (I can tell you right now that you do not lose a million brain cells every time you have a beer.)

Today we know that the brain does not stop developing in adolescence, but continues to add neurons well into adulthood. For senior executives who were always told that you can't teach an old dog new tricks, it's not true. Science has verified the amazing plasticity of our brains, a term meaning brains are able to grow and evolve to the end of our lives, enabling us to acquire new skills continually.

Brain Science

Knowing this and watching the world spin more toward a knowledge economy, it follows that we ought to do everything we can to improve that most critical asset inside our heads. In fact, management guru Peter Drucker called for continuous learning because most of us will work into our 70s by choice or to afford retirement. Drucker demonstrated continuous learning and a work ethic into his 90s.

In recent years, scientists have used tools such as the CAT, PET, and MRI scans to observe real-time brain activity. In a CAT scan the brain is viewed in cross-section as if taking a slice of the brain at any desired angle. A PET scan is sensitive to a radioactive tracer that emits bursts of energy that the scanner records. The MRI records a picture of radio signals given off by the brain as a person lies still in a magnetic field while being bombarded with radio waves.

Despite all our seeming sophistication, we remain virtually hardwired to predetermined patterns of thinking in many situations. This can be good and bad. Overconfidence is one example of the "bad," and we will dig into why this is so later. In decision making, emotion is unconsciously called in and improves our conclusions.

We Have Dog Brains!?!

For decades scientists thought we were all fully rational decision makers. That is, they assumed we made decisions that reflected simple cost/benefit analysis and our own self-interest. Now they use

MRIs and know that our brains encourage us at times to cut our noses off to spite our faces.

Scientists now tell us that we operate in the sphere of "bounded rationality." That is, we have the ability to make rational decisions, but our mental processes limit the power of our brains to make them. Experiments such as the Ultimatum Game have proven this. The MRI appears to show back and forth banter between the ancient parts of our brain with the newer parts that make us civilized. In genteel terms, the civilized part does not always prevail.

An *HBR* article, "Decisions and Desire," says this another way. "We have dog brains, basically, with a human cortex stuck on top, a veneer of civilization."[1] Let us return to the Ultimatum Game where at times you can almost hear that dog brain growling.

In the Ultimatum Game, a player receives $10 and is told to split it with the second player. The player with the money offers a split. The other player accepts or rejects the offer. If rejected, neither player gets anything. This is the game equivalent of cutting one's nose off to spite one's face, but it happens often. Researcher Alan Sanfey discovered why.[2]

When the receiving player feels that an unfair offer has been made, Sanfey observed activity in the brain's cognition areas (dorsolateral prefrontal cortex) and in the emotional part of the brain (anterior insula). Emotion lit up the MRI when the decision to reject was made, as if the rejection came forth from moral disgust.

Again, in a completely rational world, game theory would predict that any offer should be accepted, for even one dollar improves the position of the person accepting it. However, when perceived as unfair, the dog brain seems to overcome the rational brain. The more unfair the offer, the more the anterior insula becomes activated, the more akin to an animal a rational decision maker becomes.

Mr. Spock as Role Model?

Then again, the Vulcan-like maxim "all rational all the time" is not the best formula for good decisions either. Neurologist Antonio Damasio observed in studies[3] and reported in his book *Descartes' Error* that we cannot make our best decisions without input from our emotions. To conclude this, Damasio and his colleagues studied patients with injuries to the ancient animal part of their brain (limbic system). Otherwise, their brains were undamaged, providing them full IQ, memory, learning, the language. Those who faced decisions without the ability to feel the emotion were slower and seemed to struggle when making decisions.

He observed that the lack of emotion hindered intuition that enabled his uninjured subjects to perform better than injured players. Using intuition, the unimpaired players sensed trends before they became obvious, allowing them to make decisions earlier in the game that benefited their performance. Gut instinct or intuition is a critical element of successful sales management.

Mental Imaging

Many of us use the power of mental rehearsal to improve performance. The PET scan actually shows brain activity generated when we project ourselves onto the stage for that big presentation at the annual sales conference. In mentally running through the delivery of a successful presentation, the motor cortex (prefrontal and frontal lobes) areas of our brains communicate with the "little brain" (cerebellum) to pre-create and improve performance on stage. The cerebellum coordinates the movement as it compares what you thought you were going to do (according to motor cortex) with what you are actually doing and corrects the movement if there is a problem. When we practice in our minds, we create a virtual performance groove ready for playback. Remember, however, that less-than-perfect practice produces less-than-perfect playback!

As We Thinketh

Science has now seen the bright MRI colors confirming another capability we knew we had all along: positive thinking and goal-setting work. One hundred fifty years ago, James Allen wrote *As a Man Thinketh,* the classic that instructs us to consider our thoughts carefully. What we hold in our minds is what we become as people.

You should read Allen's book. Motivational speaker Tony Robbins agrees it is essential reading.

Why Goals Work

If you regularly set goals, you already know that the process works. Only recently have we come to understand the actual brain processes that enable us to achieve goals. Here is how it works. It is up to you to initiate the goal process by determining what it is you want to achieve. Next, you consider alternative paths to your goal and decide upon which one to take. You lock in an image of the completed goal and review your progress to maintain motivation and adjust your path to stay on track.

This is another imaged brain process brought about through the interplay of the prefrontal and frontal cortex in conjunction with the cerebellum. Successful speakers like Tony Robbins and successful writers like Robert Fritz, the intellect behind structural thinking, underline the importance of imaging the result of a goal in your mind. You assure yourself that the goal is what you want, and you know you will recognize it when you achieve it. The goal achievement process creates a virtual mental groove.

Fritz describes the goal process as bringing a desired creation into being.[4] The energy to achieve the creation results from a tension we set up between our goal and current reality. When we appreciate this discrepancy between where we are and where we want to be, we can create a tension in our brains that works like a stretched rubber band to power us toward our goal.

Understanding how the brain fuels our drive to goals explains why people without goals are like ships without rudders. Their behavior and results are observably different from those who hold the right thoughts and have clear goals. This raises an interesting corollary in the negative to Robert Allen's assertion that we become what we hold in our minds. As a sales executive, when you begin to think you are in trouble, you will be if you are not already. Sales managers with hangdog minds broadcast their thinking and demonstrate it through their behavior. Remember that professionals do not wear their emotions on their sleeves. You don't need to feel motivated or psyched up to do your job well. You just do it.

The rigors of the job can be bruising, causing less mentally tough managers to procrastinate if they do not "feel" motivated. Things are the way they are no matter how you feel about them. Professional sales executives do their jobs well whether they are motivated or not. Emotion (motivation) and professionalism are two different things. I have not found any research claiming brains do not work just because you are not motivated. Giving in to low motivation is giving in to an emotional response.

Zoom out with your mind to see yourself in a bigger context. When you do this, you are practicing what psychologists term observing your ego at work. When you tell yourself that real professionals can work however motivated they feel, you are strengthening muscles of your emotional intelligence.

There Are No Limits

How aggressive should one's goals be? I do not believe you should limit yourself to what you *think* you can do. You should go for what you truly want. You want what you want, and you will never know if you can achieve it until you try. As a kid, I wanted to be President. I made some progress as I reached Massachusetts' third highest constitutional office. The experience was valuable, but I lost my taste for politics and changed my goals. At the time I set the goal, however, even advancing as far as I did would have been an aggressive goal. Becoming President was an outrageous goal!

Tracy Goss wrote *The Last Word on Power*,[5] and I highly recommend it. She makes an eye-opening case for setting impossible goals. She writes powerfully and without stealing her thunder, let me relate a thought about goals and the magic of context.

Say your goal is to become vice president of sales at a $10 million company. This goal confines your mental model to thinking and acting within that context. Perhaps you would envision a small office with three or four salespeople. Your view of reality would reflect consistent expectations for your earnings, performance of your employees, and behavior in your daily job routine.

Now suppose your goal is to become vice president of sales for an $8 billion company. You are now mentally living in a very different context. Your behavior will comport itself to be consistent with an up-and-comer looking to earn a mega-salary and a seat on the corporate jet. These were impossible sights in the earlier context where your thinking was a function of your situation. Context is everything, as you will see repeatedly in our journey together.

For some additional brain self-improvement exercises, read Dr. Richard Restak's book *Mozart's Brain and the Fighter Pilot*. It is entertaining and provides 28 interesting exercises to improve your brainpower.[6]

CHAPTER 18

Evolution in Sales Management

It is the nature of man as he grows older to protest against change, particularly change for the better.

JOHN STEINBECK

Evolutionists describe how we adapt to our changing environment as survival of the fittest. If a caveman heard rustling behind a bush, he would draw upon the extent of his powers of prediction to assess his situation and act. He had little room for error, because if his intuition was incorrect, he would be lunch. Likewise, today's sales executive's success depends upon his or her intuitive powers to predict what is rustling behind the figurative bush in order to earn lunch or be lunch.

Caveman and salesman demonstrate other survival parallels. Neither can dodge the requirement to make high-stakes judgments with only ambiguous or incomplete information. Intuition prompted hunters when time came to migrate with the herd for the winter. Likewise, the sales executive watches the herd in her market to monitor cycles in her product line. Like it or not, predicting the future is an essential skill for both. Cave dwellers who could not

179

predict threats suffered shorter life spans. The sales managers with the same inadequacy suffer shorter job tenure.

The better each honed his intuition, the longer he survived and prospered. People learned that in changing environments, actions are situational and must change constantly to fit new realities. This requirement for flexibility and the pressure to make quick decisions obviates the luxury that more analytical thinking tools might provide. The requirement then and now is for adaptation to new challenges.

Making Your Age Work for You

Between the ages of twenty and forty we are engaged in the process of discovering who we are, which involves learning the difference between accidental limitations which it is our duty to outgrow and the necessary limitations of our nature beyond which we cannot trespass with impunity.

W. H. AUDEN

In the *Power of Impossible Thinking*,[1] Wharton researchers caution us that our career experience is itself a context where we must be aware of our real and perceived strengths and weaknesses. Self-awareness in our career context improves our odds of continued success. Young in their career, new sales managers bring less experience and intuition to their jobs. This makes them less valuable than senior sales executives. However, what they do bring is an openness to learn. Given this, a younger manager is not burdened with old baggage of how things were in different times.

Over time, the young manager acquires the experience and intuition that are the foundation for his or her peak career years. At career maturity, there is a subtle trend toward career demise. Researchers believe that this is due to a decline in our openness to see and embrace continuing change in our environment.

Implication for Young Sales Managers

George Orwell said, "Each generation imagines itself to be more intelligent than the one that went before it, and wiser than the one that comes after it." It is self-evident that someone on new terrain tends to be open to discern more than another to whom the landscape is old hat. Hence, this is one advantage of the new, usually younger sales manager. The void of experience implies an openness to consider new ways and means of succeeding in the job. However, if the inexperienced manager is unable to implement them, valuable insights provide little value to the field. It takes time for the new manager to become seasoned and hone his or her intuition. When that manager has the ideas *and* the capability of implementing them successfully, he or she achieves maximum value to the organization.

Implication for Senior Sales Executives

As Thoreau admonishes in *Walden,* "A man is wise with the wisdom of his time only, and ignorant with its ignorance. Observe how the greatest minds yield in some degree to the superstitions of their age." Mature career executives have a mirrored situation to the up-and-comers. You are valued for your intellectual capital and intuition. You bring judgment to the party. You can see the long-term implications of nearsighted decisions. You know what happens when you delay personnel actions that you know you should take. You are also aware that your greatest strengths can also be your greatest weaknesses, particularly as you mature. Just as a rookie manager comes to her job with a presumption of inexperience and hence less capability, you often face a presumption that you are resistant to the new and unwilling to change.

I remember a senior sales manager who pushed his people through many late nights and some weekends to reach an ambitious objective. To demonstrate his genuine appreciation, he brought the team a box of doughnuts. This person was out of touch with his younger sales force. They saw him as cheap and unappreciative of their sacrifice.

During a search for a new CSO, a CEO told me, "I don't want some guy recycling twenty-year-old sales techniques." To evade that perception, your conscious task is to be open to seeing new things and using them. Otherwise, you may become the person the CEO was describing. Confidence and experience are valuable until you begin to shoehorn old ideas into a new context where they no longer fit. Once perceived this way, you are cooked.

Managing salespeople well requires understanding them well. Implicit in this is an appreciation for their diversity and generational differences.

Four Generations

There is no hard-and-fast archetype of a person of any generation. Sociologists, however, like to identify some trends and similarities that may pertain to the people who work for you. These general tendencies may be helpful in working with the four generations represented in today's workforce.

Table 18.1 provides the breakdown of our workmates.

Veterans are those employees born in or before 1945. Now in their 60s and up, they are so-called traditionalists who inherited values from parents who grew up through the Great Depression, World War II, and the Korean War. Sociologists characterize them as hard working, loyal, patriotic, and conservative. Most have been in the military. They are comfortable with a hierarchical, top-down organizational structure. Because of this experience, they may be reluctant to speak their minds.

Veteran sales managers may encounter conflict in managing younger groups, since Veterans have more affinity for rules and procedures. A Gen-Xer looking for flexibility in working hours would conflict with this style if the manager managed strictly by the

TABLE 18.1 Four Generations

Veterans	Born before 1945
Baby Boomers	1946–1964
Generation X	1965–1980
Millennials/Generation Y	1981–1994

rules. Rules and procedures mean less to Gen-Xers. A sales manager who is not computer savvy could be seen as a relic of the Stone Age by Gen-X and Gen-Yers.

An AARP survey reported that more than 66% of workers now 45 to 74 plan to work beyond their typical retirement age.

Baby Boomers are the largest component of today's workforce. Born from 1946 through 1964, they are currently in their 40s to 60s. They grew up in a time of great growth, optimism, abundant jobs, and idealism. They compete hard and play hard with an optimistic view that they can overcome almost any difficulty.

Baby Boomers may not understand Gen-Xers' lack of company loyalty and frequent job changes. In turn, Gen-Xers will not appreciate any lectures relating to the personal values of Baby Boomers. To communicate effectively, Baby Boomers should keep their comments strictly to business issues.

Gen-Xers were born from 1965 through 1980. Today they are in their late 20s to early 40s. Gen-Xers grew up in times when company loyalty was on the wane. They have observed recessions, downsizings, corporate and social turmoil. Social institutions such as marriage have weakened as they grew. Not surprisingly, they are more independent and self-reliant than Baby Boomers.

"Generation X is much more skeptical and cynical than its predecessors, and they desire balance between work and their personal life."[2] This generation typifies "the brand called you." They desire growth, improving their personal skills, and taking risks including entrepreneurship to achieve their goals.

Millennials, also called "echo-boomers" and "Generation-Y," were born between 1981 and 2001. There are 76 million of them, a generation nearly as large as the Baby Boomers! Millennials are graduating from college and have begun to enter the work force.

Obviously, they represent a large, emerging market with new needs. This generation made the iPod a mainstream product. It is confident, enjoys friendship in the workplace, and, having grown up in the digital age, is unafraid of technology.

They may be young; however, they will resent less-than-equal opportunity to toss their ideas and solutions into the pot. Older managers can connect with Millennials by demonstrating good listening skills and reserving judgment on generational behavior and interests they may not appreciate. Properly motivated, Millennial sales reps and managers will provide a competitive edge in identifying and penetrating emerging markets.

CIA Advice for Continuing Career Success

Business is not the only sector working on intergenerational communication and management. Interestingly, the CIA has a problem with its senior analysts similar to some senior sales managers. Many assumptions they had in the past are outmoded today. Every generation locks into its own mindset, often believing that the old values no longer hold and that they are privy to insights unknown to others. Generational differences are just one reason change is difficult.

All of us are overconfident in our judgments and perceptions as individuals. It is enormously difficult to know exactly when what we cling to no longer holds. How can we see when we ought to change our beliefs? Here is a piece of advice provided to CIA senior managers to help them recognize when that time has come:

> By paying attention to their feelings of surprise when a particular fact does not fit their prior understanding, and then by highlighting rather than denying the novelty. Although surprise made them feel uncomfortable, it made them take the cause (of surprise) seriously and inquire into it . . . rather than deny, downplay, or ignore disconfirmation (of their prior view). Successful senior managers often treat it as a friendly reminder and in a way cherish the discomfort surprise creates. As a result, these managers often perceive novel situations early on and in a frame of mind relatively undistorted by hidebound notions.[3]

Superwoman and Other Dysfunctional Models

Good swimmers are oftenest drowned.

THOMAS FULLER (II), *GNOMOLOGIA*

Look at these self-defeating sales manager archetypes. No matter what our generation, most of us have watched caricatures like these. What happened to them?

> *Superwoman.* This new sales manager enters with a great flash of bravado. She declines help and in fact gives the impression that she needs no one's help. She doesn't get any. Instead, people just lay in the weeds giving her enough rope to hang herself or wait for her to burn out or get promoted.

> *The Gunslinger.* This tough guy comes to town determined to show everyone he means business. His first order of business is to shoot everyone who may or may not have been responsible for the situation that brought him to town. Then, he brings in his own deputies as replacements. Unfortunately, it will take the gunslinger a couple of years to rebuild all the intellectual capital he put on Boot Hill. He'll be there himself soon enough.

> *The Answer Man.* This new sales executive arrives knowing just what needs to be done. He is unencumbered by any of the facts of the actual situation. The plan worked before, and it will work again, dammit. Everyone quickly learns what the new plan is and assumes a position that this too shall blow over. The Answer Man is so certain that he is right that he leaves no room for flexibility to accommodate the realities of his new company.

> *The Old-Timer.* Here is the old pro, once a golden boy, who believes that he has surely "been there and done that." He has thirty years experience and knows all there is to know. Unfortunately, he missed the last twenty years of what there was to learn. Relying on his first ten years, most of his experience no longer fits. His talk is confident, but he is just not facile enough for today's business environment. The company will demonstrate that it is just as stubborn as he, when it marches him out the door.

> *The Peter Principle.* Ms. Peter Principle has stepped up to assume more responsibility than she can handle. Not only does she manage to become the sales executive, but she also adds marketing to her empire. In a large company with many challenges, she is unable to focus adequately on any of them. She

acts busy, and she is. But rather than leading the organization ahead, she's swamped and bailing water furiously to stay afloat in the here and now.

The Coattail Bandit. You can hear the Coattail Bandit galloping in from headquarters sent by her mentor. Perhaps, she has scant sales management experience. No matter, she's getting her ticket punched as she continues climbing the corporate ladder. "I'm from headquarters, and I'm here to help." She's "fireproof" until her mentor leaves. Then the dogs have at her. She follows her mentor out of the company or returns to headquarters staff. It takes a year to turn around the mess she made in the field.

There are several recurring themes in these road-to-failure examples.

Failure of Humility

It is risky to assume command with ruffles and flourishes like General George Patton. Even with his spectacular results, eventually he was sacked because of his lack of humility. Most often, as with Patton, it is people rather than results that cause career demise. When you arrive, your people are already well aware of problems that exist, and they have a remarkable ability to hear and accept the truth of a situation. They know that there are no easy solutions and that you will need their support. What they want and need is a leader. And what a leader needs to succeed is a committed team.

Overconfidence

Research regularly demonstrates that we are overconfident of what we think we know. Moreover, even when we encounter information that demonstrates an error in our thinking, we tend to ignore it. Additional studies show that even when we are aware of our tendency for overconfidence, we continue to demonstrate overconfidence just the same! Overconfidence causes us to set or agree to unrealistic expectations for ourselves—and everyone else.

The Unpardonable Sin

Repeatedly, our interviewees told us that the most common fatal flaw of CSOs is overpromising and underdelivering. Once on this slippery slope, a well-meaning CSO has nominated himself as the Monkey-in-the-Middle. Pack your bags, you'll soon be out. We heard it so often ourselves that it bears repeating. Overpromising and underdelivering is—other than stealing and moral or ethical lapses—is the single worst mistake you can make.

The Board, CEO, Finance, Operations, Production, and everyone else rely on what you tell them about sales. When you provide bad numbers, you look bad. The worst of it is they look bad because of you. They will not let you get away with it for long. It is better to predictably hit a more modest commitment than miss it altogether.

Remember, when you fail to deliver on your promise, you forfeit your stock in trade as the sales leader: your credibility. What value do you have for them if they cannot rely upon what you tell them?

CHAPTER **19**

The CEO and Sales Force Success

*A real executive goes around with a worried look
on all his assistants' faces.*

VINCE LOMBARDI

Just as there are archetypal styles of sales executives, so there are model CEOs. Two that concern you most are:

- The sales-oriented CEO
- The technically oriented CEO

Why is this so critical to you? Unless you fit with the orientation of your CEO, your tenure may be a struggle and relatively short.

CEOs we interviewed who come through sales on their way to the top believe their experience is a blessing to sales and marketing. This is mostly true. They tell us also that CEOs without a sales pedigree don't know what they don't know, as it were. Technically oriented CEOs often see sales as a straightforward function without much nuance. It is sales' job to bring in the revenue assigned to them. Period.

The sales-oriented CEO understands the complexities involved. Under either CEO, either you deliver the numbers or you are out.

However, having a work-style match with your CEO makes all journeys more pleasant.

While the technically oriented CEO does not second guess you and look over your shoulder, he does require that you make him comfortable with your approach. If you are the type who spends most of your time in the office handy to your CEO, you are already in harmony. He wants to know that you are always there watching the store for him. Be certain your reports are timely and detailed. Your forecasts must be accurate, as your CEO cannot fathom how you could be a competent CSO with inaccurate forecasts.

Evolved and Unevolved CEOs: Hurd vs. Fiorina at HP

There is another important axis on which to view your CEO. One of our experts termed this as "evolved" or "unevolved." A CEO, like any unevolved manager, is limited by a narrow scope of interest. One could argue that the primary focus for Carly Fiorina during her days as HP's head was, well, Carly Fiorina. In her later book, she blamed her woes on the machinations of others. Apparently, she remains unevolved.

Mark Hurd next assumed the reins and was swept into the HP Board scandal early in his tenure. He could have blamed others, but instead ceaselessly uttered *mea culpa*. Obviously, he demonstrated an emotional maturity that he was a team player who could be counted upon to shoulder his own share of the burden. He did not look for a scapegoat. This demonstrated that Hurd was an evolved player whom his managers could trust. Hurd and Fiorina are archetypes of the CEO behaviors just discussed.

Fiorina was fired, leaving the sales force a mess. Hurd arrived with eleven levels between him and the customer. He found half the sales force comprised of nonsales personnel. Hurd appears to be the salesman's salesman. His people perceive him—and he perceives himself—as HP's top sales officer. Where Fiorina may have been off making a speech, Hurd was in the office on the phone to work customer problems. From our interviews with insiders, we learn that it's not unusual to find Mark Hurd virtually huddled with a sales team or leadership of a key account. He may not be physically present, but he uses technology to join and chips in his ideas like any other member of the team. That is a strategic advantage for an HP sales team. When the team needs additional resources or better position-

TABLE 19.1 Hurd vs. Fiorina at HP

	Fiorina	Hurd
Background	Operations and sales background.	25 years with NCR in sales and sales management. 49 years old—entered the workforce in 1980.
CEO orientation	Planning, vision.	Sales.
Actions speak louder . . .	Bought 2 Gulfstream jets.	Sold 2 Gulfstream jets.
Focus	Personal legacy. Acquisition of largest competitor.	Revitalizing sales. Reducing eleven levels between CEO and customers.
Sales force time	Less than one-third of time spent with customers.	Now spending 40% of time with customers.
Responsiveness to sales needs	Took months to process new hire requests.	Business units make their own decisions.
Organization of sales	Centralize sales; give them all the products for one-stop customer shopping.	Realign sales with the business units. Develop expertise in a solution area.
Personal visibility	Very high. Hollywood friends. The new HP way. She is the message.	Work behind the scenes. The HP way. Tried to avoid magazine covers.
Goals	Splashy growth. Splashy acquisition of Compaq.	Rebuild HP legendary sales force competence.

ing, the team can count on him to deliver. Table 19.1 compares the styles of Fiorina and Hurd.

The point of this comparison is to contrast styles, not make value judgments. CEO styles come in and out of vogue. The critical issue is understanding how to work with whoever the boss happens to be.

If you reported to Hurd, would you employ a "be visible and available in the office" strategy? Hardly. Hurd would want you intimate with your sales opportunities. He'd rather know you were in the field with your team than supporting him by standing in wait in a nearby office. If a problem arose, and you were unavailable, he would handle it himself.

I can guess that Fiorina was too busy or traveling and thus unable to grab a hot customer call. She would expect you to keep those problems contained. After all, it is your job. Hurd is reachable with an email directly. Fiorina had processes, forms, and handlers that would take days to get through.

Will either CEO bend to your preferred management style? Certainly not. It's your responsibility to assess their needs, attitudes, and experience to serve effectively as CSO. Only a nonevolved, one-dimensional CSO would deny the importance of teamwork and perspective at the expense of a parochial ego.

Predictability

This gets to the crucial currency of predictability. Everyone desires predictability. No one likes surprises, particularly embarrassing surprises that damage credibility. Think about the importance of the concept of predictability.

Nearly everything we do, we do in an effort at predictability. We may leave early for the office to miss the traffic. How do you feel when your easy drive turns into stop-and-go traffic? We go to a particular restaurant looking forward to perhaps the best calamari in town. This time they are out. We plan to send our children to the best schools we can. Doing this, we predict happier lives for them. We bring home two dozen roses. Why? We predict the effect they will have. Even going to the refrigerator for a cold beer is an action predicted to bring anticipated satisfaction. Predictability is nice; surprise is not.

My advice for dealing with your CEO, customer, rep, peer, or anyone else is to build a reputation for being a predictable partner, colleague, supplier, or boss. The concept of being that predictable person will require a different promise to each person. The value of your predictability will vary by person, too.

Predictable Failure

A CEO of a technology company shared this example of how his own Sales VP disappointed him before the board within months of joining the company. Ben, the new Sales VP, told the board he planned to open five new offices and hire twenty new reps to staff them. Six months later, he updated his progress. One board member questioned the meager results apparent from the company's significant investment in sales growth. Without much thought, Ben jumped to the defense of his new reps. Because he failed to predict the time required to ramp up the new branches, the board member assumed that that results would have become evident after six months. Ben was demonstrating, at the expense of his future credibility with the board, how much he still had to learn to become a competent Sales VP.

Fortunately, his CEO had been a Sales VP himself and stepped in to help Ben. He told the board of his own experiences bringing new offices on line. In particular, he stressed the need for a ramp-up time of twelve to eighteen months to evaluate a new location. The board agreed to wait another six months before evaluating results; however, Ben had already hurt his credibility. His CEO saved the day, but Ben would bear scars from the skirmish.

It is essential that the board and CEO understand lag times. If a new sales team needs twelve to eighteen months before it becomes productive, say so. That way, you will develop their trust by demonstrating predictable honesty.

In a major judgment lapse, Ben made the mistake of trying to defend poor interim results. He should have reminded the board of his warning that satisfactory results would take longer to produce. Now the board has had a new perception of him. He failed to display the courage that he once exhibited. Now he's a dissembler.

CHAPTER 20

Perception Sticks Like Glue

*Once upon a time a man whose ax was missing suspected his
neighbor's son. The boy walked like a thief, looked like a thief, and
spoke like a thief. But the man found his ax while digging in the
valley, and the next time he saw his neighbor's son, the boy walked,
looked and spoke like any other child.*

LAO-TZU, PHILOSOPHER

I sat beside the VP of sales and marketing observing a regional sales
manager's (RM) team review. The manager and five reps presented
their plans enthusiastically. Actual sales were awful, but it was clear
the sales reps were well positioned and in the right accounts. The
team was doing the right things; it was simply too early to see
results.

The region was newly created and the reps newly hired or trans-
ferred in. The manager was experienced; however, in his eagerness
to showcase the reps by holding the bad news to the end, he made
a judgment error. As the team results became clear, the VP whispered to me, "He hasn't sold enough to pay for the lunch we ate."

We drove back to the airport debriefing on the meeting. It was
certain the RM erred by holding all the bad news to the end. The VP,
of course, kept a running total on his own, so that that he was not

surprised when the actual numbers were revealed. What upset him was his own view that the regional manager was being "cute," trying to soften the real message by plying him with hospitality and upbeat presentations.

We had both attended the same meeting, yet our perceptions of the team were 180 degrees apart. He wanted to fire the regional manager. He agreed that the team was still in ramp up, and it was too soon to expect significant results. He knew that on a rational level. Nevertheless, at the same time, his emotions were flaring, because he believed the regional manager tried to dupe him.

By the time our plane landed, we had a plan. He would observe progress and results for six months, long enough to close sales already in the pipeline. We would also take a closer look at the RM's day-to-day management activities. I returned to spend two days observing and talking with the RM. Next, I created a coaching plan for the RM.

As I worked with the RM more closely, I was more certain of his competence. However, back at headquarters, each time the regional manager's name came up over the next few months, even though the news was encouraging, the VP retained his earlier emotional position. Progress reports were not enough to turn change his perception.

In the seventh month, the VP convinced himself that he had misjudged the RM. The RM's results catapulted him into number one in the country. Although the VP was wrong about his sales manager, that is not the point of this case. We are all wrong at times. I tell the story to illustrate how resistant the mind is to change. The VP ultimately convinced himself to change his perception. He was immune to proof other than what he used to convince himself—the six-month actual results.

Iceberg Perceptions

This story is worth remembering when someone holds a misperception involving you. Perceptions do not melt away like ice cubes. They are more like icebergs where the potential for damage is unseen.

At an AT&T dinner for new sales managers, several of us dined with senior executives so exalted and removed that we knew of them only by reputation. It was a time for proper table manners and careful conversation. Across the table, I observed a nonstop, one-way conversation between one of my new colleagues and a suave EVP, who was getting an ear full. The executive was gracious and listened politely as the new hire, aided by several scotches, told him how to run the company. I had a ringside seat to see how a negative perception forms as fast and deadly as a strike by a viper. At the end off the evening, the EVP, stood, walked around the table, and whispered into my boss's ear, "You see that guy Johnson over there? Get rid of him."

There is another discouraging similarity between a bad perception and a snakebite. There is no assurance that you will recover. Some bites are always fatal. Nevertheless, we are optimists, so we should try to cure negative perceptions of us held by others. To do this we must understand what we are up against.

Perceiving the Risks

Here is an actual situation a perceptive sales manager would have avoided in the first place. Bill Ralston (not his real name) was a new hotshot sales manager from outside the industry. The CEO believed that Bill's training and experience at one of the world's most respected companies would overcome his lack of industry knowledge. About six weeks into the job, the CEO invited Bill to meet the Board.

After pleasantries and a glowing introduction by the CEO, Bill outlined his strategy to turn the sales force around. Then he presented his sales outlook for the next quarter. He knew it was risky to make predictions so early in his new tenure. However, he wanted to demonstrate to the board that the CEO's confidence in him was well placed. Personally, he wanted the Board to perceive him as "in command." He committed that the sales slide would be arrested and reversed.

His pledge was risky, since he had neither industry background nor experience with the reliability of field forecasts. Even so, he decided that the last thing he wanted to reveal to the Board was the truth—that he was uncertain about sales for the quarter. However, his desire to create an image trumped his humility and better judgment.

As events played out, honesty would have been his best strategy. It always is. Contrary to Bill's assertion, revenue results would decline again. At the next board meeting, the first order of business was the sales decline in light of his forecast. What could the sales VP say? On one hand, he could admit that he had no idea why sales declined. Owning up to this explanation, he figured, would destroy his remaining credibility. Or he could say, "Wait next quarter!", reaffirming that his program was grabbing and improved results were just around the corner.

We don't need psychologists to tell us the lengths we will go to avoid pain. Like the kid caught in a lie, Bill avoided certain pain in another gamble. He had boxed himself into a corner by reaffirming himself. In retrospect, he had just reeled off enough rope to hang himself.

Sales would decline again in the next quarter and would continue to decline long after Bill was gone. Bill let his desire to be seen as "in command" get the better of his judgment to know the truth and tell the truth. The board would grow in its conviction that he was doing neither.

Flexibility and Success

Bill had also embarrassed his new CEO, who had hired him and brought him to the board with such confidence. Now the CEO wondered what the board was thinking about his own judgment and prospects of returning the company to profitability. However, the CEO never shared these personal concerns with Bill. What would be the point?

Too late, Bill wished he might have wound the tape back to that first board meeting. He would have told the Board that his interests were the same as the Board's, namely to turn around slumping sales. The Board was well aware of the sales situation and naturally hopeful that Bill could turn things around for all of them. As sales vice president, they deferred to his judgment as he took action to turn things around. They were hopeful and supportive, as was the CEO. They all had a right to the truth, and this should have been obvious to Bill.

If you sat on that board, how would you perceive Bill? He delivered false hope that the company was turning around. Perhaps, some members of the board communicated this assessment to friends, colleagues, and bankers. Now their judgment might be called into question. Could they believe anything he told them? Now, everyone had a problem.

Certainly one moral of this story is the need to maintain flexibility until enough data is in to see the trend clearly. Bill could have maintained credibility and bought himself time had he not foreclosed his options. He might have told the Board that he was proceeding with a particular plan he believed showed promise. However, if he did not achieve the results he expected, he had backup plans B and C. Flexibility is critical for long-term success. Short-term bravado is a one-time only pleasure.

Know the Truth

Gerry Spence, the attorney who always wins his cases, tells us that we should not present anything to a jury—and this certainly applied to the board—unless we have prepared thoroughly.[1] Spence leaves nothing to chance, including the confidence he displays because he knows he is always speaking with honesty. Once people get even a scent that you are not telling them the truth, you will lose them. Spence does not hide what may come out later and hope it will not. He defended Imelda Marcos, former first lady of the Philippines, from charges of spending government funds on herself. He preempted his opponent by telling the jury himself that she had about 3,000 pairs of shoes. As always, he went on to win his case.

Observing Our Own Perceptions

The series of drawings below illustrate how prone we are to swift creation of perceptions, and then how difficult it can be to change them. If you happen to start looking at the drawing below from the upper left, you will continue seeing the man for some period until your mind convinces itself that something different is developing. Those who begin at the lower right at the end will have a similar result. In *retrospect,* we see everything clearly!

(Drawing concept devised by Gerald Fisher)

Try another example. Unless you have seen this before, it will leave you with another demonstration of how resistant your own mental models are to change. Read the following:

Most people do not "get" it the first time. I have seen people read these pyramids three and four times carefully before they spot the double articles.

Let us complete this important discussion of information and perception with a final illustration. If you still doubt that your subconscious can alter your conscious perception, count the number of Fs in the following:

FINISHED FILES ARE THE RE-

SULT OF YEARS OF SCIEN-

TIFIC STUDY COMBINED WITH

THE EXPERIENCE OF YEARS . . .

I received this unattributed piece over the Internet with the notation that the average person finds three Fs. In fact, there are six. For whatever reason, most of us have difficulty spotting the combination "of."

Unless you are a *rara avis,* your mind operates with its own perceptions without your permission or awareness. This is a critical insight to have in your job:

- We usually see what we expect to see.
- More information may have little or no value.
- Mindsets form quickly, change with difficulty.

Therefore, when you attempt to change a mindset held by another, you have to "be loaded for bear." Ideally, present information that the other person can objectively analyze to test the validity of his or her position. Opinions, hearsay, or anecdotal information, no matter how compelling to you, are easily discounted because they are not easy to test.

You will add to your credibility by involving an independent third party. If you are persuading a skeptical CEO, for example, it is helpful to have your VP of Marketing or other independent colleague along to support your position.

CHAPTER 21

FAQs: Frequently Asked Questions

Hiring

Q. I've heard that it's a best practice not to hire people who remind us of ourselves. What's your opinion?

A. All of us have a tendency to like people who remind us of ourselves. Be aware that a well-briefed candidate can easily manufacture attractive similarities between the two of you. The value of the interview isn't in discovering that you both love the Thousand Islands for family vacations. The value is in identifying the skills and attitudes required for success and, if abundantly found, to attract the person to your organization.

Remember that we are also attracted to people who are tall and/or good-looking. They walk into the interview under a halo of attributes we subconsciously award them (described below). Unconsciously, we become enchanted, before we know a thing about them. Researchers refer to this phenomenon as "priming." Priming can also trigger negative unconscious judgments based upon our biases and prejudices.

As I noted, these predispositions happen before we can prevent them. The trick is to neutralize them by being aware of priming and its effects. Therefore, always stay with your predetermined interview process. There are obvious legal reasons why we must be consistent from one interview to the next. I always use a preplanned set of behavioral questions that ask a candidate to recall actual sales situations. I will ask for a story that demonstrates how his or her unique sales skills drove the sale. Likewise, I ask for an example of a situation where he or she failed, why, and what he or she would do differently now. Focus your thinking to the conscious rational level. Take a closer look at the facts, remembering that when we are primed, we are apt to overlook information that does not support our perception. Finally, it is important to have several qualified candidates so that you have options.

Q. Assuming they are qualified, is there an advantage to hiring attractive sales people?

A. Studies have shown repeatedly that whether you are in sales or running for President of the United States, the better looking you are, the more successful you tend to be. You will win more elections and pocket greater financial rewards than your less attractive competitors. One study showed that people who are more attractive earn 12 to 14% more than less attractive coworkers.[1] Even attractive criminals get breaks based on their good looks. Juries tend to give them significantly lighter sentences and even convict them less often.

Influence researcher Robert B. Cialdini puts it clearly: ". . . It is apparent that good-looking people have an enormous advantage in our culture. They are better liked, more persuasive, more frequently helped . . . and believed to have greater intellectual capacities."[2] You can see why the plastic surgeon (Chapter 6) understood that beauty has economic value worthy of improving his sales targeting.

All this being said, the candidate should be a match for the demographics of the assignment for which you have hired him or her. Competence trumps attractiveness.

Overconfidence

Q. Why is it that salespeople are often overoptimistic with their forecasts?

A. Overconfidence is an abiding characteristic of human nature. People are almost always more optimistic than their past experience would justify. I read of a poll in which Americans were asked about whether they would end up in the top 1% of all wage earners. Forty percent of them said that they would! One reason for overoptimism is the failure to adequately consider what might go wrong when they hope for all to go right. At other times, people fail to consider even rudimentary probability of something happening, as was the case in Chapter 11 when the company fired seven sales managers.

Q. Why is it that sales reps defend their forecast even when presented with contrary information?

A. Part of the reason stems from our characteristic stubbornness and desire for consistency. Almost everyone finds it difficult to change once he or she has made a decision. From that point, we subconsciously overweight new information that supports our decision and underweight unsupportive information. If you ever discuss politics, the phenomenon of stubbornness becomes quickly apparent!

It is not a profound insight to say that Republicans and Democrats make stubbornness an art form with researchers finding people of both parties highly reluctant to fairly evaluate new information that has the potential to change their point of view. These were not subjective observations, for researchers used MRI machines to gather physical evidence. When people have their minds made up, evaluative brain activity just stopped when people heard information contrary to their current belief.

Sometimes the problem is simple miscommunication. We define our terms subjectively. To one person, a *high probability* that a deal will close may mean over 50% probability. To someone else, a high probability of closing can mean 90% certainty. Successful sales managers make certain that everyone on their team speaks the same language.

Q. Is consistency an issue in negotiation?

A. Dr. Daniel Kahnemann, a Nobel Prize winner, believes there is an "anchor" effect. He observes that first impressions tend to be lasting (anchored) in evaluating a new acquaintance and in situations dealing with money and negotiation. For instance, once a price is quoted, people tend to accept it unconsciously as the point around which the negotiation revolves.

This phenomenon adds more risk to situations such as bidding on a new piece of business where you have very little information. It is human nature; but worse, it is unconscious human nature. Counterintuitively, instead of greater anxiety, we mistakenly feel some measure of comfort when someone at least puts a stake in the ground. Manipulative people know this and may throw out a figure that stakes it to their advantage. Plan and prepare your opening position for all the important items of the negotiation. This gives you room to negotiate to your desired settlement point and prevents you from exceeding your walk-away position.

Changing Territories

Q. Is changing the rep in a sales territory likely to help or hurt sales?

A. This depends on several factors. As a guideline, even apparently well-worked territories of star performers continue to produce business when taken over by a new pair of eyes. Carryover of business in the pipeline is one factor. Another is that successful salespeople tend to ignore new account potential because they have sufficient opportunity and comfort at their best accounts. They do not have to prospect. A viable territory mismanaged by an incompetent rep is an obvious target for development.

CEO

Q. What are some of the key things a CEO can do to help the sales force?

A. First, the CEO should review any Hindenburg Omens identified by sales leadership. Then, assuming agreement that it represents a potential point of failure for the sales program, commit to partner with sales to monitor and improve the problems.

CEOs without sales experience should keep an open mind to identify situations and forces that even a great sales force cannot overcome. Recall the partnership of Pliny and Emperor Trajan (Chapter 9), when they discovered that there are times when markets change and cannot be changed back.

A CEO should understand that both good and bad markets exercise profound influence on the behavior of the sales organization and thus the results of any sales leader managing within it.

Another area where a CEO can be particularly helpful is evaluating the interdependencies of sales and other departments. Smooth internal operations are essential for everyone's success, and that happens only when the CEO demands it and rewards teamwork. More silos exist than CEOs are willing to admit to. CEOs will surprise themselves with wasted sales resources required to navigate internal silos.

Finally, but not exhaustively, a CEO can also see that sales gets the funding for resources required to succeed. This includes adequate investment in technical support, training, and adequate territory manpower to retire assigned quotas.

Q. Sometimes a CEO or other senior executive tells a sales manager what he or she thinks should be done to improve sales. Sometimes that opinion seems uninformed, even foolish. What can be done in situations like this where we are told to take certain actions that we know will not help?

A. The directives that I hear most often in this category are "fire that guy!" or something similar to "I want everybody putting out two proposals a week . . . or opening two new accounts a week, etc." We have grown up all our lives doing what authority figures tell us to do. One of IBM's patron saints, Thomas Watson, Jr., pointed out that unquestioned authority goes too far. In his book *Father, Son and Company*,[3] he wrote about an extreme reliance on authority airline officials call "Captainitis." This refers to taking the word of some expert—be it an airplane captain, doctor, or professor—without question. In World War II Watson's father researched a tragic accident due to the tendency to do what the captain tells you to do even if it is patently stupid: A general in the pilot's seat was breaking in a new co-pilot who took the right-hand seat in awe of him. The general hummed a tune to himself and bobbed his head up and down as he occasionally looked over to his co-pilot. The co-pilot mistook the head bobs for silent commands. As the plane rolled at full throttle down the runway, the general repeated his unconscious head bob to the co-pilot who believed the general was signaling him to retract the landing gear. In Watson's report, it was obvious to both pilots that the plane was well below take-off speed. Nevertheless, the co-pilot was so reliant on authority that he raised the gear even in the face of certain catastrophe. This extreme case raises the question, Why do we comply with direction that clearly will not work? If you as the sales manager are confident of your position, it is your fiduciary responsibility to clearly communicate the consequences in language that the CEO understands.

Learning

Q. Why is it that some people in my organization seem rarely to learn from their mistakes?

A. All of us have a sense of self-esteem that is damaged when we make mistakes—some of us more than others. It is an accepted psychological tenet that when we an encounter failure, such as a loss of a major account, we tend to attribute the loss to circumstances, bad luck, or even alpha particles. Rarely do our unconscious egos accept personal responsibility that we screwed up.[4] Our unconscious mind works so powerfully to protect us that we are almost certainly unaware that our ego is presiding over a monumental cover-up. This happens outside of sales, too.

I read a study that evaluated sportswriter bias in a number of daily newspapers that covered a series of sporting events. When their local team won, there was a tendency to attribute the success to the skills and attributes of the players on the team. This happened in 75% of the articles that explained winning as a function of superior skills. When the favorite local teams lost, only 55% of the time was there an attribution of the loss to mistakes by the local team.

Losses tended to charged off to forces beyond our control. This is one of the reasons to consider Peter Drucker's practice of keeping a written record of decisions and looking at them years later to maintain a sense of the balance between luck and skill in our management lives.

It's just as much a cover-up when we overattribute the role of personal skills and derring-do in our successes. We rarely attribute success to luck or circumstances that would have favored anyone.

People are not lying when they do this. They are subject to their own best belief of the truth, as orchestrated unconsciously by their egos.

In the extreme, unchecked ego manipulation leads a sales manager or CEO to an unwarranted overassessment of his or her own skills. Humility is an engaging character trait no matter how successful you become. Otherwise, how will you learn from your mistakes?

Loss Reviews

Q. What is your opinion of loss reviews?

A. They are great when held under no preconceived conclusions of guilt or innocence. Unfortunately, my experience is that this is rarely the case. We all have this hankering to learn "who shot John"—that is, to find some cause for every result, even if we must manufacture one. I have never heard of a loss review concluding that an account was lost by chance or bad luck.

We know from earlier chapters that preexisting perceptions and prejudices are difficult or impossible to overcome. Even without prejudice, there are other difficulties inherent in loss reviews. For instance, a common fallacy is the notion that we managers ought to be in control of a particular situation. Many studies have shown the common belief that one controls one's situation. I found one study particularly fascinating: The participants were told to try to score as many points as possible by working with the lever on the box they had in front of them. The participants tried a variety of tactics with the lever before settling on the particular patterns of control they felt were most effective in racking up points. For instance, some would make a couple of quick pulls on the lever to exhibit a style to control point production. At the end of the experiment, it was revealed that the participants had no control whatsoever over the amount of points that were awarded. Points were awarded in an arbitrary manner. Nevertheless, participants maintained certainty that their activities had the effect of producing points during the experiment.

In another extraordinary experiment, half the participants chose their own lottery number. The other half received a random assortment of numbers. Then, researchers asked all participants to set the price for which they would sell their $2 lottery ticket. Incredibly, those who chose their own numbers wanted an average of $9 to part with them compared to the $2 price of those who had random-numbered tickets. We all know that lottery numbers are perfectly random, that any number is as likely to be drawn as another. It is astonishing that one group felt that they were exercising some control over the winning numbers on their lottery tickets. This is an extreme example of self-attribution, but no more extreme than maintaining that anyone maintains control over all the random occurrences in a bid contest.

Earnings and Tenure

Q. What are the average earnings in sales management?

A. For all managers, the U.S. government says the 343,000 and growing population of sales managers is second only to CEOs. Most sales managers earn an average of $92,610.[5] As a side note, from 2002–2012 the U.S. Labor Department projects 168,000 new positions and 21 to 35% growth.

Q. What is the average tenure of the sales executive?

A. I suspect it is the shortest of any senior officer position. I found one study on the subject. This was a 2002 survey of Silicon Valley sales vice presidents. According to this source,[6] the average tenure of the sales vice president was *only 12 months*—down from an 18-month average in the prior year's survey results.

Decision Making

Q. With all the built-in unconscious biases we have as sales managers, are we more likely to be manipulated and make some poor decisions? Any ideas on preventing this?

A. Sales management is about making decisions. Most of the time you must make decisions without all the information you'd like, in a changing environment, usually in a short time, under uncertainty and often for large stakes. You will make mistakes and have to take this as a "given" in the job. It bears repeating that 75% of the time anyone in your position would make the same decision given your circumstances.[7]

TABLE 21.1 How Simple Guidelines Help Us Make Smarter Decisions

Old Way of Deciding What to Bid (One Decision at a Time)	Thin-Slicing (Your Guideline)
Everyone applies his or her own criteria based upon his or her own experience to place bets.	There is a uniform set of criteria determined after study and input from your most successful producers and best thinkers.
No easily or consistently applied method is used to examine if the decision to invest resources was a good or poor one.	The opportunity "meets" or "does not meet" the predetermined criteria. Metrics are clear and easy to review. There is less opportunity for unconscious factors (such as bias) to influence the decision.
With nothing more important to do, the rep may bid on marginal opportunities because some chance is better than none. He or she may also engage an opportunity merely to fulfill an activity metric or to look busy.	If the opportunity does not pass, a rep cannot work on it without his or her manager's override of the algorithm. The opportunity now receives scrutiny.

One way to cut down on bad decisions is use heuristics. Use tools like thin-slicing to create guidelines for routine decisions. That way, you become less susceptible to bias and manipulation that are likely by deciding similar situations one at a time. Table 21.1 demonstrates how simple rules can make us smarter—and save us time. The table summarizes some of the material in Chapter 4, Sales Controls and Policies.

Q. What is the worst of the Hindenburg Omens? Where does the sales force fit in the mix?

A. I attended an excellent sales management program at Northwestern's Kellogg School and heard a lecture by Professor Lou Stern, an expert in distribution. Dr. Stern put some math on the board, which I noted and very much agree with (see Table 21.2).

TABLE 21.2   Importance of a Good Product

Product Quality		Distribution Quality		Company Result	
0	×	1	=	0	Great distribution, poor product = Failure
1	×	0	=	1/2	Great product, poor distribution = some success
1	×	1	=	3	Synergy and success

There is no success without a good product. It is at the center of your strategy and answers the question: Why do people give us money? A company with a great product and relatively poor distribution will achieve some success. Once the company perceives a product as lacking value, why would anyone buy it no matter how impressive its distribution? This is not a theoretical question. Many fine sales executives have lost their jobs because of CEOs who fail to understand that a new sales manager will not improve results. This is why it is so critical for you to understand the adequacy or inadequacy of a company's product line before accepting a sales leadership role. Be certain that it is possible to succeed!

Best Wishes for Success

Thank you for buying my book. I wrote it to discuss topics not commonly discussed in sales management books and to apply advances in neuroscience, psychology, behavioral economics, decision making, and other skills such as intuition to sales management. We understand how and why sales management is different from all other corporate responsibilities. We know why people in other departments don't cooperate with or even like salespeople. We have explored Hindenburg Omens and considered other challenges to our success. We know how to leverage our time and improve success by using tools such as thin-slicing. We face challenges, but none that we cannot manage. I encourage your feedback and would enjoy hearing your stories.

Notes

Chapter 1

1. Arthur Miller, *Death of a Salesman* (New York: The Viking Press, 1958), 81.
2. Jerome A. Colletti & Mary S. Fiss, "The Ultimately Accountable Job: Leading Today's Sales Organization," *Harvard Business Review 84* (7/8), (Jul/Aug 2006), 124, 185–190.
3. Fred Hassan, "Leading Change from the Top Line," *Harvard Business Review, 84* (7/8) (Jul/Aug 2006), 90.
4. Sun Tsu, *The Art of War,* Samuel B. Griffith, Translator (Oxford, UK: Oxford University Press, 1963), 138.
5. See also Robert Fritz, *The Path of Least Resistance for Managers: Designing Organizations to Succeed* (San Francisco: Berrett-Koehler Publishers, 1999).

Chapter 2

1. Sun Tzu, op cit., 138.
2. For a more detailed discussion of carryover and sizing, see Andris A. Zoltners, Prabhakanant Sinha, & Greggor A. Zoltners, *A Complete Guide to Accelerating Sales Force Performance* (New York: AMACOM, 2001), 70–110.
3. Gardiner Morse, "Decisions and Desire," *Harvard Business Review,* 00178012, Jan 2006, Vol. 84, Issue 1 <http://web.25.epnet.com>, February 2006.

4. C.W. Lamb, Jr., J.F. Hair, Jr., & C. McDaniels, *Marketing,* (Cincinnati: South-Western, 1996), 728.
5. Ibid.
6. Katherine Hobson, "Making Those Choices About Right and Wrong." *U.S. News & World Report, 138* (2/28/2005). Accessed May 2006, from <http://web12.epnet.com >
7. Susan Powell Mantel, "Choice or Perception: How Affect Influences Ethical Choices among Salespeople." *Journal of Personal Selling & Sales Management, 25* (1) (Winter 2005), 43(13). Thomson Gale, *Professional Collection* (Goodnow Public Library) (18 December 2005) <http://find.galegroup.com/itx/infomark>

Chapter 3

1. Rosabeth Moss Kanter, *Confidence: How Winning Streaks and Losing Streaks Begin and End* (New York: Crown Business, 2004), 111.
2. See: Gary Klein, *Sources of Power: How People Make Decisions.* (Cambridge, MA: MIT Press, 1998).
3. J. Edward Russo & Paul J.H. Shoemaker, *Decision Traps: Ten Barriers to Brilliant Decision Making* (New York: Fireside, 1989), 67–74.

Chapter 4

1. Malcolm Gladwell. *Blink: The Power of Thinking Without Thinking* (New York: Little, Brown and Company, 2005).

Chapter 6

1. Clayton M. Christensen. *The Innovator's Solution: Creating and Sustaining Successful Growth* (Boston: Harvard Business School Publishing Corporation, 2003), 73–75
2. Peter F. Drucker, *Management Challenges for the 21st Century* (New York: HarperCollins, 1999), 29.

Chapter 7

1. Raymond Kurtzweil, *The Singularity Is Near* (New York: Penguin Group, 2005), 10–45.
2. Frederick W. Smith, "Deregulation and the Global Market Revolution." Speech presented to Cato Benefactors, 2005.

3. Erin Anderson & Bob Trinkle, *Outsourcing the Sales Function: The Real Costs of Field Sales*. (Mason, OH: Texere, 2005), 13.

4. Ralph E. Anderson, Alan J. Dubinsky, & Rajiv Mehta, "Sales Managers: Marketing's Best Example of the Peter Principle?" *Business Horizons, 42* (1) (Jan-Feb 1999).

5. Ibid.

6. Sales Vantage.com Accessed November, 2005, from <http://salesvantage. printthis.clickability.com/pt/cpt?action=cpt&title=The+Wild%2C<http:// salesvantage.printthis.clickability.com/pt/cpt?action=cpt&title=The+Wild %2C+Wild%2C+West+of+Sales+Forecasting+%3A+Forecasting&expire= &urlID=8900131&fb=Y&url=http%3A%2F%2Fwww.salesvantage.com %2Fnews%2Fforecasting%2Fwild_west.shtml&partnerID=1009>+Wild %2C+West+of+Sales+Forecasting+%3A+Forecasting&expire=&urlID=89 00131&fb=Y&url=http%3A%2F%2Fwww.salesvantage.com%2Fnews %2Fforecasting%2Fwild_west.shtml&partnerID=1009>

7. Gallup poll, cited in Anderson et al., op. cit.

8. M. Marchetti, "Whatever It Takes." *Sales & Marketing Management* (December 1997), 29–38.

9. Anderson et al., op. cit.

Chapter 8

1. Richard Restak, *Mozart's Brain and the Fighter Pilot* (New York: Harmony Books, 2001).

Chapter 9

1. Corporate Strategy Board, *Stall Points* (Washington, DC: Corporate Strategy Board, 1998). In Clayton M. Christensen, op. cit., 5.

Chapter 10

1. Raymond Kurtzweil. Author's notes from speech presented to George Gilder Forum. Sun Valley, California, June 2005.

2. Peter L. Bernstein, *Against the Gods: The Remarkable Story of Risk* (New York: Wiley, 1996).

3. Jack D. Wilner, *7 Secrets of Sales Management: The Sales Manager's Manual* (Boca Raton, FL: St. Lucie Press, 1998), 13.

4. Tom Lombardo, "Outlook." *The Futurist* (January-February 2006).

Chapter 11

1. *Management Focus* (November–December 1984), cited by Paul Shoe-maker in *Winning Decisions* (New York: Doubleday, 2002).
2. Malcolm Gladwell, op. cit., <http://www.gladwell.com/blink/blink_excerpt2.html>
3. Richard Restak, *Mozart's Brain and the Fighter Pilot* (New York: Harmony Books, 2001), 158.
4. Quoted in Darrell Huff, *How to Lie with Statistics* (New York: W.W. Norton & Company, 1982).

Chapter 12

1. Title of science project by Nathan Zohners.
2. Accessed from <http://en.wikipedia.org/wiki/Best_practice> February, 2007.
3. Jeffrey Pfeffer & Robert I. Sutton, *Hard Facts, Dangerous Half Truths and Total Nonsense: Profiting from Evidence-Based Management* (Boston: Harvard Business School Press, 2006), cited in *Wall Street Journal* review 5-16-06.
4. Kevin Patterson, "What Doctors Don't Know (Almost Everything)," *New York Times,* 2002, cited in Pfeffer & Sutton, op. cit., 13.
5. *Science Daily,* "Danger in Marathon Runners Drinking Too Much Water." Accessed March 29, 2007, from <http://www.sciencedaily.com/releases/2000/05/000503183723.htm>
6. Fred Cohen & Associates, accessed February, 2007, from <http://all.net/journal/netsec/1997-09.html>. For a discussion of the issue see <http://www.cerias.purdue.edu/weblogs/spaf/general/post-30/>
7. Quoted by Colletti & Fiss, op. cit.
8. Michael Roberts, *Working Knowledge: The Power of Ordinary Practices.* Accessed September 20, 2006, from <http//hbswk.hbs.edu/item/5492.html>

Chapter 13

1. Accessed March, 2007, from <http://www.meaningoflife.i12.com/intuition.htm>
2. Gary Klein, *The Power of Intuition* (New York: Doubleday, 2003), 4.
3. Jerry Wind, Colin Crook, & Robert Gunther, *The Power of Impossible Thinking: Transform the Business of Your Life and the Life of Your Business* (Upper Saddle River, NJ: Wharton School Publishing, 2005), 176.

4. William J. Attenweiler & Frank R. Kardes, "Kahnemann's Contributions and Their Continuing Impact." *Kentucky Journal of Economics and Business, 61* (2003). See also Robin M. Hogarth, *Educating Intuition* (Chicago: The University of Chicago Press, 2001), and Gary Klein, *Sources of Power: How People Make Decisions* (Cambridge, MA: MIT Press, 1998).

5. Klein, op. cit., 156.

Chapter 14

1. Paul Slovic, *Behavioral Problems of Adhering to a Decision Policy.* Unpublished manuscript quoted by Richard Heuer, CIA.

Chapter 15

1. Dr. Daniel Kahnemann won the Nobel Prize in 2002 for his research in behavioral economics and in particular his findings concerning human judgment and decision making under uncertainty. For more information see <http://nobelprize.org/nobel_prizes/economics/laureates/2002/>.

2. Naomi I. Eisenberger & Matthew D. Lieberman, "Why Rejection Hurts: A Common Neural Alarm System for Physical and Social Pain." *Trend in Cognitive Sciences, 8* (7) (2004). Cited in James Montier, "Emotion, Neuroscience and Investing: Investors as Dopamine Addicts," *Global Equity Strategy,* January 20, 2005.

3. Roy F. Baumeister & Mark Muraven, "Self-Regulation and Depletion of Limited Resources: Does Self-Control Resemble a Muscle?", *Psychological Bulletin, 126* (2) (March 2000) 247.

4. Amos Tversky & Daniel Kahnemann, "Judgment under Uncertainty: Heuristics and Biases." *Science, 185,* (Sept. 27, 1974), 1124–1131.

Chapter 17

1. Gardiner Morse, "Decisions and Desire," *Harvard Business Review, 84* (1) (January 2006).

2. Alan G. Sanfey et al., "The Neural Basis of Economic Decision-Making in the Ultimatum Game." *Science 300* (5626) (June 13, 2003).

3. Damasio Bechara, "Deciding Advantageously Before Knowing the Advantageous Strategy." *Science 275* (1997).

4. Author's notes from Organizational Structure class with Robert Fritz, Newfane, Vermont, 2004.

5. Tracy Goss, *The Last Word on Power: Executive Reinvention for Leaders Who Must Make the Impossible Happen* (New York: Doubleday, 1996).

6. Restak, op. cit.

Chapter 18

1. Cited in Wind, Crook, & Gunther, op. cit.

2. Christine Wilson & John Foltz. *Feed & Grain, 44* (5) (Aug/Sep 2005), 54–61.

3. Quoted by Richards J. Heuer, Jr. from Daniel J. Isenberg, "How Senior Managers Think," in David Bill, *Decision Making: Descriptive, Normative, and Prescriptive Interactions* (Cambridge, UK: Cambridge University Press, 1988), 535.

Chapter 20

1. Gerry Spence, *How to Argue and Win Every Time: At Home, at Work, in Court, Everywhere, Every Day* (New York: St. Martin's Press, 1995).

Chapter 21

1. D. Hammermesh & J.E. Biddle, "Beauty and the Labor Market." *The American Economic Review, 84* (1994), 1174–1194, in Cialdini.

2. Robert B. Cialdini, *Influence: Science and Practice* (Boston: Allyn and Bacon, 2001), 150.

3. Thomas J. Watson, Jr., *Father, Son and Company: My Life at IBM and Beyond* (New York: Bantam, 2000).

4. Cordelia Fine, *A Mind of Its Own: How Your Brain Distorts and Deceives* (New York, W.W. Norton & Company, 2006), 6-29.

5. Wages & Employment Trends, <http://online.onetcenter.org/link/summary/11-2022.00>

6. Accessed from <http://www.warnersalesarchitects.com/articles.htm>

7. Klein, op. cit.

Bibliography

Anderson Ralph E., Alan J. Dubinsky, and Rajiv Mehta. "Sales managers: Marketing's best example of the Peter Principle?" *Business Horizons, 42* (Jan-Feb 1999), 19.

Anderson, Erin, and Bob Trinkle. *Outsourcing the Sales Function. The Real Costs of Field Sales.* Mason, OH: Texere, 2005.

Cialdini, Robert B., *Influence,* 4th ed. Boston: Allyn and Bacon, 2001.

Clemen, Robert T. *Making Hard Decisions.* Belmont, CA: Duxbury Press, 1991.

Farson, Richard. *Management of the Absurd: Paradoxes in Leadership.* New York: Simon & Schuster, 1996.

Gigerenzner, Gerd, and Peter M. Todd. *Simple Heuristics That Make Us Smart.* New York: Oxford University Press, 1999.

Goss, Tracy. *The Last Word on Power: Executive Re-Invention for Leaders Who Must Make the Impossible Happen.* New York: Doubleday, 1996.

Gross, John. *The Oxford Book of Aphorisms.* New York: Oxford University Press, reissued 2003.

Harvard Business Review. Special Issue. "Decision Making: Better>Faster> Smarter." (January 2006).

Heuer, Richards J., Jr. *Center for the Study of Intelligence.* Washington, DC: Central Intelligence Agency, 1999.

Hogarth, Robin M., *Educating Intuition.* Chicago: The University of Chicago Press, 2001.

Huff, Darrell. *How to Lie with Statistics.* New York: W.W. Norton & Company, 1982.

Jones, Eli, Steven P. Brown, Andris A. Zoltners, and Barton A. Weitz. *Journal of Personal Selling & Sales Management, 25* (2) (Spring 2005), 105(7).

Klein, Gary. *The Power of Intuition.* New York: Doubleday, 2003.

Klein, Gary. *Sources of Power: How People Make Decisions.* Cambridge, MA: MIT Press, 1998.

Mantel, Susan Powell. "Choice or Perception: How Affect Influences Ethical Choices among Salespeople." *Journal of Personal Selling & Sales Management* (Winter 2005).

Montier, James. "Emotion, Neuroscience and Investing." *Global Equity Strategy* (January 20, 2005).

Morse, Gardiner. "Decisions and Desire." *Harvard Business Review, 84* (1) (January 2006).

Olson, Eric M., David W. Cravens, and Stanley F. Slater "Competitiveness and Sales Management: A Marriage of Strategies." *Business Horizons* (March, 2001)

Reason, James. "Human Error: Models and Management." *The Western Journal of Medicine, 172* (6) (June 2000), 393.

Restak, Richard. *Mozart's Brain and the Fighter Pilot.* New York: Harmony Books, 2001.

Rubin, Louis D., Jr. (Ed.). *Writer's Companion.* New York: HarperCollins, 1997.

Russo, J. Edward, and Paul J.H. Shoemaker. *Winning Decisions: Getting It Right the First Time.* New York: Currency Doubleday, 2002.

Russo, J. Edward, and Paul J.H. Shoemaker. *Decision Traps. Ten Barriers to Brilliant Decision Making.* New York: Fireside, 1989.

Shiller, Robert J., *Irrational Exuberance,* 2nd ed. Princeton, NJ: Princeton University Press, 2005.

Sternberg, Robert J. (Ed). *Why Smart People Can Be So Stupid.* New Haven, CT: Yale University Press, 2002.

Stevenson, Howard H., with Jeffrey L. Cruikshank. *Do Lunch or Be Lunch.* Boston: Harvard Business School Press, 1998.

Sun Tzu, *The Art of War.* Griffith, Samuel B., Translator. Oxford, UK: Oxford University Press, 1963.

Wilson, T.D. *Strangers to Ourselves: Discovering the Adaptive Unconscious.* Cambridge, MA: Harvard University Press, 2002.

Index

221

About the Author

Dr. Wayne M. Thomas is a sales management expert, consultant, speaker, and author.

Wayne is CEO of Thomas & Company, Inc., a management consultancy he founded in 1994 to help sales organizations make midcourse corrections and develop sustainable long-term strategies. He has extensive experience with a variety of firms such as AT&T, Sprint, SAS Institute, Nortel Networks, Novell, and Siemens.

Earning his Doctor of Business Administration (D.B.A.) degree in 1999, Wayne has also completed the Columbia Graduate School of Business Executive Program and the Kellogg Graduate School programs in Sales Management as well as the Columbia Executive program in Marketing. He holds an MBA and has studied at Oxford University, England, completed information technology training at the Cambridge Learning Center at MIT, the AT&T Executive Development Program, and the IBM sales training and marketing curriculum, and has a Certificate in Data Communications from Northeastern University.

He served as a Branch Manager and Division Sales Manager at AT&T and as a Program Manager at IBM. As a sales representative, he earned IBM's highest sales award, the Golden Circle. While at AT&T, he was named American Marketing Association Boston Marketer of the Year and earned the President's Award for building the top performing sales organization in New England. He was chief marketing and sales officer for two channel companies, which he grew nationally to a sales organization of 300 representatives. One company (UST) earned the Boston Chamber of Commerce Small Business of the Year award, the other (CTC) achieved recognition as an *INC Magazine* fastest growing small public company.

He was Editor of the *TIA Channel Intelligence Report*, a member of the TIA Enterprise Board of Governors, and on the board of the Enterprise Communications Association. He writes regularly for industry publications including *Phone+, Fat Pipe,* and *Computer Telephony*. He is also the author of the *Sales Agency Handbook*, published by Nortel. Wayne speaks nationally on marketing, sales management, and strategy topics at industry and company forums.

He has served as Executive Councilor to the Governor of Massachusetts, the state's third ranking constitutional office.

His outside interests include hiking, golf, and enjoying family life with his wife Susan and daughters Emily and Kathryn.

You can contact the author at *Wayne@ThomasAndCompany. com* or www.ThomasAndCompany.com.